"This book explores the mundane invisibilization of male violence against women through an examination of the killing of Hélène Legotien by Louis Althusser. Francis Dupuis-Déri highlights Legotien's life and work, challenging the erasure of women who are victimized by male violence. A sharp focus on this one case provides a vibrant example of the operation of masculine solidarity so central to the process of hiding male violence against women and gendered violence in plain sight."

Alan Sears, author of *Eros and Alienation: Capitalism and the Making of Gendered Sexualities*

"*Killer Althusser* is a brilliant book. Dupuis-Déri deftly deploys the case of Hélène Legotien, who was murdered by philosopher Louis Althusser—with little consequence to his fame or stature—to lay bare the persistent and violent effects of male supremacy. This vital book is a burst of justice and love and deserves the widest audience possible."

James K. Rowe, associate professor, School of Environmental Studies, University of Victoria

Hélène Legotien photographed in Corsica in the 1950s.
Source: Louis Althusser's archives / IMEC.

SALLE HÉLÈNE
LEGOTIEN-RYTMANN
Résistante et sociologue
Victime de féminicide en 1980 à l'ENS

DÉFENDONS
NOS Sud Solidaires
RETRAITES

En mémoire de
HÉLÈNE LEGOTIEN-RYTMANN
sociologue et résistante
assassinée par son mari (L. Althusser)
en 1980 à l'ENS
ON N'OUBLIE PAS
ON PARDONNE PAS

Graffiti on the window and door of the Raymond Aron Room at the École normale supérieure de Paris, since renamed the Hélène Legotien-Rytmann Room. Author(s) unknown. Source: Photo courtesy of Lucie Rondeau du Noyer.

Killer Althusser

The Banality of Men

Francis Dupuis-Déri

Translated by Mélissa Bull

Between the Lines
Toronto

First published in French by les Éditions du remue-ménage as Althusser assassin. La banalité du mâle © Francis Dupuis-Déri et les Éditions du remue-ménage, 2023.

This edition published in 2025 by
Between the Lines
401 Richmond Street West, Studio 281
Toronto, Ontario · M5V 3A8 · Canada
1-800-718-7201 · www.btlbooks.com

Library and Archives Canada Cataloguing in Publication
Title: Killer Althusser : the banality of men / Francis Dupuis-Déri ; translated by Mélissa Bull.
Other titles: Althusser assassin. English
Names: Dupuis-Déri, Francis, 1966- author | Bull, Melissa, 1977- translator
Series: Provocations (Toronto, Ont.)
Description: Series statement: Provocations | Translation of: Althusser assassin. | Includes bibliographical references.
Identifiers: Canadiana (print) 20250109905 | Canadiana (ebook) 20250110539 | ISBN 9781771136778 (softcover) | ISBN 9781771136785 (EPUB)
Subjects: LCSH: Althusser, Hélène—Public opinion. | LCSH: Althusser, Louis, 1918-1990—In mass media. | LCSH: Homicide—France—History—20th century. | LCSH: Women—Violence against—France—Public opinion. | LCSH: Victims of crimes in mass media. | LCSH: Violence in men—France—Public opinion. | LCSH: Public opinion—France—History—20th century.
Classification: LCC HV6535.F7 D8613 2025 | DDC 364.152/3092—dc23

Cover and text design by DEEVE
Printed in Canada

We acknowledge for their financial support of our publishing activities: the Government of Canada; the Canada Council for the Arts; and the Government of Ontario through the Ontario Arts Council, the Ontario Book Publishers Tax Credit program, and Ontario Creates. We acknowledge SODEC for their financial support of the translation of this book. La traduction de cette œuvre a été rendue possible grâce au soutien financier de la Société de développement des entreprises culturelles (SODEC).

Contents

Introduction

I remember asking him the same question over and over again: how could I have killed Hélène?
—Louis Althusser, *The Future Lasts a Long Time*

Hélène Rytmann was born in 1910 to a Jewish family. Her youth, if we are to trust Louis Althusser's account of it, was marked by two major tragedies. When she was thirteen years old, on the Rytmann family doctor's recommendation, Hélène administered a lethal dose of morphine to her father, who had terminal cancer. The following year, once more at her doctor's recommendation, she performed the same service for her mother.

During World War II, Hélène, a member of the French Communist Party, joined the Resistance in Lyon under the name Legotien. She would later publish her essays on the sociology of culture and economy with the same name. When Hélène Legotien met Louis Althusser, he was teaching philosophy at the prestigious École normale supérieure on rue d'Ulm in Paris. Hélène and Louis were romantically involved for about thirty years. They married in 1976, one year after Hélène's retirement.

At the beginning of the Cold War, Hélène was an activist in the Soviet Peace Movement until her comrades expelled her from their party ranks, accusing her of Trotskyism or of having been paid off by the Gestapo or the Intelligence Service. Her husband confessed to being among those who had voted to have her ousted.[1] While Althusser's standing as a Marxist philosopher was upheld, he was psychologically unstable to the point of requiring frequent psychiatric hospitalizations. Hélène Legotien managed concerns for the state of her husband's health from loved ones, who did not express any similar interest in her own welfare—something she experienced as an "intolerable injustice."[2]

Sometime around 9 a.m. on November 16, 1980, in their lodgings at the École normale supérieure, Louis Althusser massaged Hélène Legotien's neck. Then he strangled and killed her.

Within a matter of hours, the authorities at the École normale had the murderer admitted to the Hôpital Sainte-Anne. There Althusser remained for several years, until he moved to a new apartment in Paris. He died October 22, 1990.

Immediately after Althusser murdered Legotien, an explanatory theory of madness emerged in the public discourse. The examining magistrate, Guy Joly, appointed three psychiatric experts to assess whether Althusser had been in a "state of insanity" at the time he committed the murder and whether he was sufficiently conscious to understand the charge of voluntary man-slaughter. Althusser himself confided that he "appre-ciated both the competence and the independence" of the expert opinions that led to his case's dismissal;[3] the legal proceedings against him were ultimately dropped. On November 19, 1980, France's daily newspaper *Le Monde* published an article on the case, presenting "the hypothesis of psychopathology that can explain a murder."[4]

This psychological account of Althusser's murder included no sociological, political, or feminist analyses.

It is this public discourse, which had the effect of exonerating the killer, that I wish to examine. My research is based on a cross-analysis of the murderer's own words—Althusser expounds upon his motives at length in his autobiography, *The Future Lasts a Long Time*—as well as upon perspectives explored in newspaper articles and magazines published after he committed murder and after the publication of his autobiography, as well as on scholarly works. In this corpus, I consider the discourses of journalists, editorialists, columnists, and intellectuals—most often men—as well as psychologists and psychiatrists, and including specialists in economics or contemporary French literature.

The objective is not to distinguish or compare the various registers of discourse involved in this case but rather to reveal how, together, they express the same certainty; namely, that Legotien's murder may be explained by examining her killer's psychology. This interpretation has the effect of depoliticizing the case to the point that it exonerates the murderer. As the discourse progresses, it becomes all the more clear that the Althusser case acts as a social revealer,[5] as by revisiting this crime, and particularly by examining the public discourse around the crime, we can see how a network of male protection and solidarity established to benefit the killer makes it possible to highlight the "hiding strategies" of male violence against women.[6]

Feminist Insights

Before discussing Althusser's murder of Legotien and the aftermath of his crime, we should examine the feminists' analysis of the discourse of men's violence against women—specifically, studies on the media's representation of "domestic tragedies" or "crimes of passion," as they were called before the term "*féminicide*" (femicide) was taken up by French journalists around 2019—and named word of the year by the *Petit Robert* dictionary, which added the definition of the word in 2015.

In 2021, a conference entitled Femicides in France in the Nineteenth Century: Socio-history, Challenges, and Representations was held in Paris, accompanied by an exhibit of photographs by Camille Gharbi ironically titled "Acts of Love," which can be viewed online.[1] Research carried out in the English-speaking world indicates that media narratives of femicides generally focus on the murderous man rather than on his murdered partner or ex-partner.[2] Not only are the victims' stories minimized, but they may even be held responsible for their own deaths. The murderer's responsibility, meanwhile, is often downplayed. Each case is treated piecemeal—as an isolated event—which obfuscates our understanding that murderous male violence is a social phenomenon that is reproduced year after year. Journalists, when treating one story, rarely mention similar cases—even when several are the subject of articles within the same newspaper issue or have occurred just a few days apart. Included among the explanations that diminish the murderer's responsibility are depression and his partner's desire to leave him—the poor man couldn't bear it, so he killed her. It's worth noting that these narrative tropes exist in both the media discourse dealing with Hélène Legotien's murder by her husband as well as in the killer's own autobiography.

A study conducted in France found that journalists regularly use "psychological or even psychopathological reasoning" to explain "crimes of passion," especially when the murderer is a middle-class white man. Journalists will, however, proffer sociocultural causes when the murderer is a man of foreign origin, particularly if he is Muslim,[3] as the latter's murderous violence is then understood as the expression of an archaic, patriarchal culture—his committing murder might be described as an "honour killing," as if it were a kind of cultural ritual, whereas this term is never used to describe a white man's violence.[4]

Several feminist scholars specializing in male violence against women have shown that public discourse of women tends to ignore any reference to social gender relations, an attitude they consider to be part of the "process of depoliticization."[5] In their research, psychologists Annik Houel and Patricia Mercader and sociologist Helga Sobota distinguish between two types of "psychological theorizations."[6] Reasons for the murder are either "sought in the criminals' childhood"—particularly with regards to an absent or violent father or a domineering mother—or "criminals are subject to a kind of psycho-logical diagnosis" without the individual in question or their medical records ever being consulted. The public discourse communicated in the media concerning Hélène Legotien's murder fits this pattern, as does the murderer's account of his crime in his autobiography.

To better understand the political significance of the rhetoric employed for the spousal murder committed by Althusser, it is useful to examine the complementary observations of sociologist Mélissa Blais and psych-ologist Patrizia Romito.[7] Blais's work analyzes media discourse on the antifeminist mass shooting at the École Polytechnique de Montréal on December 6, 1989, when a young man shot and killed fourteen women (thirteen students and one administrative clerk) after declaring, "I hate feminists."[8] Blais notes that the media presented the terrorist above all as a "madman," despite the fact that he had explicitly stated his antifeminist political motivations. After the terrorist committed suicide on the scene, the police discovered a manifesto on his person, outlining the following prediction: "Even if the epithet 'mad shooter' will be attributed to me in the media, I consider myself a rational erudite." The media immedi-ately described him as a "mad shooter." For his part, Althusser, during the time he was known as a rational erudite, invested a great deal of energy into presenting himself as insane and therefore not responsible for the murder he had committed.

Romito has studied "psychologization" as one of the most common tactics for concealing male violence against women, arguing that it constitutes "a rejection of political analysis" that prevents us from thinking that these murders are part of a sociopolitical logic, even if the statistics are very clear on the subject.[9] "Psychologization is, therefore, in essence, a tactic of depolitization, responsible for maintaining the status quo and strengthening the dominant power . . . Psychologizing can also be used to decriminalize a particular action."[10]

Blais has outlined how the media adopted this psychologization of the École Polytechnique shooter, alongside psychologists and psychiatrists who had neither met the killer nor consulted his medical files, revealing how psychologization has the effect of transforming the "mad shooter" into a victim (he's sick, he's suffering) and to absolve him of responsibility (the cause of the attack is madness, or the root of his madness is feminism and feminists).[11] Blais's research on antifeminist discourse has revealed that these same rhetorical tactics can be found among antifeminist intellectuals and activists who both contest and denigrate feminist analyses of male violence. Blais has identified in this type of discourse the "theory of inversion," which either shifts the responsibility for violence to the victimized woman or presents the man and the woman as two equally coresponsible or "cocreators" of violence. Blais also highlights how anecdotes are often used to present the violent man as a victim of various adversities, including those his spouse may have inflicted upon him. Finally, Blais has brought to light how the rationalization process makes it possible to justify human violence by popularizing to an extreme extent more or less serious theories, supposedly based on prehistoric archeology (the "cave man era" and mammoth hunting) or biology (genes, hormones, etc.). When examining how Althusser's crime was reported, it's clear that these are simply sophisticated fabrications on the theme of psychoanalysis.[12] In addition to directing empathy towards the murderer and diverting attention from the victim, antifeminist discourse contributes to the depoliticization of male violence. It undermines the legitimacy of feminist analyses, which are reproached for being simplistic or ideological.

Blais's and Romito's reflections share similarities with the observations of British specialist on male violence Jalna Hanmer. Presented in France in 1977 and in the first issue of the journal *Questions féministes*, Hanmer stipulates that the challenge of analyzing male violence is not necessarily "the explanation of such an individual act: our central concern is the meaning, at the socio-structural level, of men's violence against women."[13]

The Social Context
of the Murder

With regards to Hélène Legotien's murder, we only have her spouse's—her murderer's—account to refer to. His autobiography, written in the mid 1980s and published in 1992, two years after his death, opens with:

> What follows, down to the last detail, is my precise memory of those events, forever engraved on my mind through all my suffering. Suddenly I was up and, in my dressing-gown at the foot of the bed in my flat at the École normale . . . Hélène, also in a dressing-gown, lay before me on her back . . . Kneeling beside her, leaning across her body, I was massaging her neck . . . The muscles in my forearms began to feel very tired; I was aware that they always did when I was massaging. Hélène's face was calm and motionless; her eyes were open and staring at the ceiling. Suddenly, I was terror-struck . . . I knew she had been strangled. But how? I stood up and screamed: "I've strangled Hélène!" I rushed out of the flat and ran full pelt down the narrow staircase with its iron handrail into the front courtyard enclosed by tall iron gates. I kept running towards the sick bay where I knew I would find Dr. Étienne who lived on the first floor

. . . I climbed the stairs four at a time, still screaming: "I've strangled Hélène!"[1]

French literary specialist Catherine A. Poisson and psychologist Vania Widmer have conducted close studies of Althusser's narrative and concluded that it is undermined by a significant problem: "Althusser is absent from the murder. The murder takes place without him."[2] If we are to believe the killer's account of what happened, he was massaging his wife, then experienced a kind of absence—almost a trance. He regained consciousness only to discover that Hélène Legotien was dead. What a surprise!

This narrative draws on the rhetorical tropes used by media when reporting on "crimes of passion." "The terms chosen to describe this moment [of the murder] as an accident, as the accident of a being subject to error and not the subject of his crime."[3] The doctor who performed the autopsy of Hélène Legotien's body nevertheless identified "fractures of the larynx."[4]

In his over-three-hundred-page autobiography, Althusser shares his personal history as a way of rationalizing the murder. He suggests that his crime can be explained by psychological and psychoanalytic motivations, neglecting any reference to gender politics or feminism. This murder, however, is neither an incredible nor an unimaginable event, particularly when considering the context of the French patriarchal system where it transpired. Indeed, feminists have clearly demonstrated that male violence against women is a social phenomenon that occurs with regularity, in addition to being the subject of important feminist mobilizations, including at the time of the murder. Along with sociologist Pauline Delage and socio-demographer Maryse Jaspard, sociologists Alice Debauche and Christelle Hamel recall that the denunciation of male violence against women was "one of the major issues raised by the feminist movement of the 1970s . . . The denunciation of the various forms of violence against women was the subject of numerous demonstrations and many militant writings—take back the night demonstrations, political trials, etc."[5] Already in 1977, three years before Althusser strangled Hélène Legotien, the journal *Questions féministes* asserted that men's violence against women often occurs within the context of a couple's relationship.[6] *Questions féministes* was founded by Simone de Beauvoir and such Marxist-trained feminists as Christine Delphy and Monique Wittig, among others.

The murder of Hélène Legotien by her husband, a Marxist philosopher and communist activist, occurred after a decade of feminist mobilization around male violence against women. Althusser, a renowned philosopher who taught scores of future intellectual stars (Étienne Balibar, Régis Debray, Michel Foucault, Bernard-Henri Lévy, Jacques Rancière) and rubbed shoulders with academic and artistic heavyweights (Paul Éluard, Jacques Lacan) is somehow completely ignorant—in his autobiography as well as in his other writings—of feminism, as either a social movement or a theory. As the "private is political,"[7] feminist analysis nevertheless makes it possible for us to understand the sociological and political significance of murder, to adopt a critical reading of the explanation put forward by the killer himself as well as by his allies, and to recall that the benefit of social protection the killer derived from his allies is not exceptional when male celebrities kill (or rape) women.

This, indeed, is what feminist philosopher Geraldine Finn proposed in her 1981 article in *The Canadian Forum* titled "Why Althusser Killed His Wife." Finn's article expresses her anger at the tactics deployed in both the English-language press and in prominent Marxist journals, such as the *New Left Review*, that this murder was treated as a matter of private life and mental illness alone, in addition to identifying the murderer as the murdered woman's victim:

> Neither Althusser, nor "France," nor the world-renowned intellectuals and revolutionaries will acknowledge patriarchy as the powerful, pervasive, and pernicious ideological state apparatus which it is; at the same time, none of them escape its effects. The specificity of patriarchy as a political ideology and as a practice was overlooked by Althusser and is constantly denied, negated, or trivialized by the intellectual and academic élite . . . As long as this continues and men refuse to take the feminist critique seriously, they will continue to reproduce the violent patriarchal social relations which they have internalized.[8]

Even today, in France, a man kills his spouse or ex-spouse on average every three days. Most of these crimes take place in their home. Hélène Legotien was one of these murdered women. The data, which is fairly consistent throughout France as well throughout other countries, including Canada, Great Britain, the United States, and elsewhere, supports the theory that a man decides to kill his spouse or ex-spouse rather than accept that she will leave him and emancipate herself from the relationship.

According to the murderer's account, Hélène Legotien told Louis Althusser she wanted to leave him a few days before he killed her. In his autobiography, Althusser notes his refusal to let his wife leave him in words that are somewhat equivocal: "Hélène stormed out violently . . . something I could not bear. To me they were like death threats (and you know how active my involvement was with death)."[9] The murderer presents himself as a victim of the woman he killed, who he deems would have threatened his survival, as a man. This is consistent with the remarks of spousal homicide experts, who indicate that "the most common reason given by men who have committed spousal homicide is the inability to accept marital separation," with the murderers declaring that they cannot "tolerate the loss of their spouse and . . . grieve the relationship."[10] In his autobiography, Althusser explains himself as follows:

> I do not know what exactly I put Hélène through (I do know, however, that I was truly capable of the most terrible things), but she told me with a determination that terrified me that she could no longer live with me, that in her eyes I was a monster and that she wanted to leave me for good. She began quite openly to look for a flat, but did not find one immediately. She then

made practical arrangements which I found unbearable; totally ignoring me, though I was still there, in
our own flat. She got up before me and disappeared
for the whole day. If she happened to stay at home,
she refused to talk to me and even to come face to face
with me . . . I was consumed with anguish. As you
know, I always experienced intense anguish at being
abandoned and especially by her, but being totally
ignored, though I was still there, in our own home,
was the most unbearable thing of all.[11]

The situation seemed dire, as he added: "She told me
there was no way out, given the 'monster' I was and the
inhuman suffering I inflicted upon her, other than to kill
herself."[12] According to the murderer, Hélène Legotien
even asked him to help her by killing her. At that time,
the couple was completely isolated, to the point where
they no longer answered the door or even took phone
calls from the therapist who was working independently
with Hélène Legotien and Louis Althusser, who was
trying to reach them because he knew the couple was in
crisis, or at least that Althusser was, having taken steps
to have him hospitalized.

Experts debate whether men who commit spousal
homicide are inherently violent or if they are intrinsic-
ally peaceful spouses capable of suddenly acting out
and killing their partner. Statistical data on the matter is
inconclusive. Theories of "cycles of domestic violence"
and "continuums of violence" have been developed by
feminist researchers to refer to situations where the murdered woman was the target of a set of violent dynamics

over the course of the relationship.[13] Althusser referred to himself as a "monster" and mentioned the "perpetual rows" that opposed him to his wife.[14] He confessed, "I was truly unbearable. My constantly aggressive and provocative behaviour wounded her deeply."[15] Their relationship, therefore, was not only conflictual, but it was one marked by violence—at the very least psychological violence. In addition, it was an unequal partnership to the advantage of the man, in terms of his professional success, income, prestige, and social influence, due to his social and emotional networks. It was neither unreasonable that Hélène Legotien wanted to leave her husband nor was it surprising that he reacted abominably to her desire for emancipation.

Psychologization and Victimization

Published posthumously, the first edition of Althusser's autobiography sold over thirty-five thousand copies. It was translated almost simultaneously in a dozen countries.[1] This book was described as a "major work of contemporary philosophy" by Olivier Corpet, one of the editors of Althusser's archives, while the newspapers hailed the book as "sincere" and a "must-read," containing "more truths than elsewhere."[2] Intellectuals even dubbed the book a "masterpiece of autobiographical literature."[3] One might also, however, read Althusser's autobiography as a rather tedious text on a literary level, revolting from a political point of view, and disgusting from a psychological perspective, given how the murderer presents himself as a victim. Althusser also reveals himself to be pretentious and conceited, comparing himself to such acclaimed philosophers as Descartes, Kant, Kierkegaard, Rousseau, and Wittgenstein. He recounts his entire life, starting at the beginning—"I was born at 4:30 a.m. on October 16, 1918"[4]—and spares us neither his whims nor any number of insignificant anecdotes, ultimately ending with an explanation of the murder as the consequence of a life marked by childhood traumas. Beyond its specifics and its multiple digressions, the sole purpose of this 576-page autobiography is to represent the murderer as someone who is not responsible for his crime.

If, while reading his autobiography, we remember that the author killed his wife, certain passages may be unsettling, such as when he reports how, upon first meeting Hélène Legotien, he was "filled with a powerful desire to serve her: to save her and help her live! Throughout our life together, right to the very end, I never abandoned this supreme mission which gave my life its meeting until the final moment."[5]

The whole is interspersed with psychoanalytic reflections that often adopt patriarchal and sexist tropes, while allowing the author to count himself among

> the greatest philosophers were *fatherless* and lived out their lives in the solitary realm of their own theory and in the lonely risk they took in relation to the world at large . . .True, I did not have a father and continued indefinitely to play the role of 'father's father' to give myself the illusion that I did have one . . . But it was only possible if I conferred on myself the essential role of the father: that of dominating and being the *master* in all situations.[6]

He concludes, "Had I not finally and truly become my own father, that is to say, a man?"[7]

This autobiography nevertheless offers compelling material if one wishes to propose a feminist analysis of marital murder and public discourses on the subject. We understand that Althusser's father—because he did, in fact, have one—embodied a patriarchal and very violent male role model. Althusser's father did not perform any domestic or parental tasks, and he subjected his wife (Althusser's mother) to sexual and economic violence, forbidding her to work for wages. He flirted with his friends' wives in front of his own, a behaviour that Althusser in turn reproduced in front of Legotien.[8]

The murderer, in addition, presents himself throughout his book as being obsessed with conventional gender identities. He evokes a grandmother who looked like "a rather masculine woman" because she urinated standing up and recalls that his colleagues accused each other of being women, even "mothers."[9] Of his adolescence, he writes: "I wasn't a boy at all, but a feeble little girl."[10] As for Hélène Legotien, he refers to her as "a *man*," a "good mother, and also a good father," adding, "We truly made love like a man and woman."[11] One may be startled again when reading certain comments in which the murderer conflates masculinity with the protection of women, describing without any trace of irony: "My successive failures reinforced my prejudice and fear which not surprisingly reinforced my doubts about my real manhood and my capacity to love a woman and be of help to her in her life."[12]

In his autobiography, the murderer portrays a masculine elite marked by machismo and misogyny. We meet a Jacques Lacan who has fallen in love with the young daughter of one of his patients; a dean of the Moscow Faculty of Philosophy who comments to Althusser, as he is about to leave the USSR, "Say hello from me to the young ladies of Paris!"; a Paul Éluard who receives

Althusser while a naked young woman lies sleeping on a sofa; an Althusser who picks up girls along Saint-Tropez's beaches and caresses the breasts of a friend's young companion he'd invited to dinner.[13] In the paragraph that explores his 1948 membership in the Communist Party, he evokes above all the memory of "a beautiful young woman in a negligé (her breasts showing)" when he campaigned door-to-door.[14] Finally, the murderer also describes why he was building up a "reserve of women":

> I did not want to run the risk of finding myself *alone one day without a woman*, if by any chance one of my women friends left me or died. This did happen on numerous occasions, and if I always kept *a reserve of women* in addition to Hélène, it was to ensure that, if by chance Hélène abandoned me or died, I would never for a single instant find myself alone. I know only too well this awful compulsion of mine caused a great deal of suffering to "my" women, and especially to Hélène.[15]

In addition to the ambiguity in his reference to Hélène's death, this is a man who believes that he owns women and that he is ready to make them suffer by playing them off against one another—even his wife—despite being aware of the pain he causes her.[16]

The book provides many options for a feminist analysis of Hélène Legotien's murder: the killer's father modelled self-centred and violent behaviour, his perception of women is sexist and macho, he reveals himself to be egocentric and violent against women, and he considers women to be his objects. That said, in his auto-biography, the Marxist philosopher conflates the violence he inflicts upon others with the violence he claims to suffer, which invariably allows him to identify himself as a victim. Evoking memories of his youth, Althusser recounts slapping a classmate: "All of a sudden, I slapped his face, though I could not explain the reason for my violent outburst." He also recalls slapping a little girl, stating, "I never knew what came over me."[17] In both cases, Althusser speaks of a sudden violence seemingly occurring of its own volition, despite the fact that he is the perpetuator of that violence, the aggressor.

Likewise, the murderer refers to himself, on several occasions, not only as a victim but as a dead person. "Having no authentic existence of my own, doubting myself to the point of believing I was insensitive, and feeling I was incapable of sustaining an emotional relationship with anyone . . . Since I did not really exist, I was simply a creature of artifice, a non-being, a dead person."[18] Following the murder of his wife, Althusser presented himself as a "disappeared" person (a term he borrowed from Michel Foucault, who uses the term in the context of civilization and madness[19]) because the dismissal of the legal case against him would have deprived him of testifying in court and therefore of providing his version of the facts. He writes that testifying would have allowed him "to remove the weight of the tombstone[20] which lies over me . . . I had to survive and learn to leave beneath the oppressive weight of that declaration, which was like a wall of silence, or as if I were dead in the eyes of the public."[21]

The author-murderer of this autobiography recalls that he was psychologically unwell in the weeks leading up to the murder. These psychologizing explanations put forth by the murderer to exonerate himself and present himself as an anguished victim were adopted by his relatives and allies, including by the doctor and the director of the École normale supérieure, immediately after the murder and later by the press.

Vania Widmer notes that, in 1992, "the press commenting on the publication of the autobiography now accepted Althusser's version of his mental illness as an explanation for the murder" and that the media's comments remained "generally quite complacent with Louis Althusser."[22] The French newspaper texts I've analyzed present the killer as a victim suffering from "melancholy," "crises," and "indefinite anguish"; prey to a "painful immensity"; and living in an "inner hell."[23] They describe Althusser as "crucified to his sorrow."[24] Amen.

In his preface to the collection of letters Althusser wrote to his wife, the philosopher's former student, Bernard-Henri Lévy, evokes the "pain" and "madness" of the man he calls his "master."[25] The editor of the "Books" section of the newspaper *Le Monde*, Jean Birnbaum, wrote a review of *Letters to Hélène*, which Birnbaum decided to open by reporting that one of his friends confided to him, after reading this collection, "It's simple, if a man sent me letters like these for thirty years, I'd let him strangle me too!" With such an introduction, it isn't surprising that the author, after a few conventional detours ("these texts are fascinating and must be recognized as such" and that they express a "dialectic between creation and destruction" where "everything happens as if the annihilation of the other and of oneself were the only way to hold the couple together"), culminates with this lyrical flight: "Only the ransacking of bonds makes it possible to found a new alliance; annihilation remains the only act of creation, *the ultimate proof of love*."[26] Here we can compare the empathetic remarks towards Althusser with those expressed about singer Bertrand Cantat after he killed his wife, actress Marie Trintignant. In both cases, the murderers are men who belong to the intellectual or cultural elite. On this subject, legal expert Lucile Cipriani explains in an article in the Montreal newspaper *Le Devoir*:

> The language of an aggressor can therefore occupy all the space, diverting attention completely from the suffering of the aggressor rather than that of the victim . . . The misfortunes of childhood, the torments of jealousy, breakups, ego wounds, the unhappiness of living and the desire to control aggressors of women are regularly described by the media . . . Why is the speech of the aggressor of a woman listened to? Why is he received with empathy by a portion of the population? . . . It is socially accepted and integrated . . . Culture provides a space for the aggressors' discourse. The aggressors' discourse not only diverts attention to their suffering rather than that of their victims, it participates in the perpetuation of violence. The invocation of one's suffering by an aggressor pursues an exculpatory purpose.[27]

This insistence on presenting the killer as a bruised and suffering being, or even as a (crucified) martyr, is clearly part of "the trend towards the individualization and psychologization of the phenomenon" of male violence against women.[28]

Worse still, Althusser is presented as being a likeable, charming person, "the sweetest and most amiable of men."[29] When discussing the murder, it would then be a question of "restoring Althusser to his fragile humanity"[30] by presenting him as a "generous," altruistic, and compassionate man who showed himself able to "listen tirelessly to others" and who had "a tremendous hunger for life,"[31] not to mention "a proud sportsman," and "a ladies' man."[32] It is not difficult to grasp how such adjectives influence the murderer's public image, given that he was profiled in such a way as to elicit empathy for this suffering, yet so sympathetic, "victim."

The newspapers echo the murderer's own theory of his crime; namely, that because in the nonsuit of a trial and given the dismissal of the judicial case, he was "condemned . . . to silence," to a "burial," thus transmogrifying him into the "living dead."[33] It is worth noting that this idea that there are two victims to a murder, with the murderer being categorized as existing among the "living dead," are common tropes in any media coverage of "crimes of passion."[34]

Widmer also concluded there was no diversity in the media discourse regarding Althusser's crime; indeed, quite the contrary, everyone agreed that madness was the cause of the tragedy. After reviewing the various studies published on the subject, authored by biographers or doctors,

Widmer concluded: "In the literature I have consulted, Althusser's madness seems to be the only explanation for the murder."[35] The only variations Widmer identified in the discourse concern the precise diagnoses of mental illness: manic-depressive psychosis, schizophrenia, paranoia, acute melancholy with suicidal obsession, hypomania, or bipolarity? It is also debated whether by killing his wife, Althusser did not *in fact* want to kill his sister (he had dreamed of it), or his mother (castrating), or his father (Oedipus), or his therapist, or himself . . .

Even psychology professor Annik Houel, one of the authors of the excellent study mentioned above, analyzing the media discourse on "crimes of passion" in France from a feminist perspective, offers a psychological explanation in an interview entitled "Femicide's Underbelly: The Althusser Case," conducted by another professor of social psychology Claude Tapia. Houel determines that spousal homicides are "an effect of the inequality of the sexes in our society" but nevertheless defines the murder committed by Althusser as a "deferred matricide"; that is, the murder of a mother by her son, by which he would have sought to "compensate for the failures of the paternal function" he would have been confronted with.[36]

And so goes the competition of such cerebral arguments to propose the most sophisticated, jargon-ridden, and abstract explanations for a straightforward marital murder. Éric Marty, a professor of French literature at the University of Paris-VII, stands out in his book *Louis Althusser, a Subject Without a Trial: Anatomy of a Very Recent Past*, published without apparent embarrassment by Gallimard's L'infini imprint, edited by Philippe Sollers, who knew Althusser personally and who also published his book *On Philosophy* under this same imprint. Marty offers this interpretation of the murder of Hélène Legotien, apparently seriously:

> Anticipating death and being dead are not the same thing, but what characterizes Althusser is precisely perhaps that he accomplished both simultaneously . . . Even more than in everyday madness, it was in murder that he was able to experience dying, that he was able to experience death both as given and as received, and that he died during his lifetime . . . Perhaps it was then his destiny as a murderer to live actively with death while suffering it. The autobiography, which was born from this murder, is nothing other than that: life seen from death . . . Thus, the intersubjective couple of murderer and victim could be described, not in the traditional form of two autonomous subjects, one active and aggressive, the other object and passive, but in a very particular intersubjective dialectic, a dialectic of the pure situation that some great novels or some great films have been able to reconstruct . . . A relationship whose fatality and tragic purity are precisely due to the fact that the murderer-victim couple is in fact one and the same person watching himself act in a mirror of flesh.

Marty adds about his book that

> the corpse's subjectivity will be discussed, it being understood, in the case that concerns us, Althusser's,

that this corpse is forever younger than a newborn, it is always-already old, tied up, swaddled, ever-watched by its mother, that is to say, by the one who took life away, as some witches do in fairy tales.[37]

This book closes with these disjointed words:

Let us salute Althusser—murderer of murderers—one last time, and consider that if the procedure of silence is, according to Kierkegaard, that of the murderer, it is also that of the hero. Of the modern hero. Of the anti-Ulysses. The one who is not betrayed only by himself. The one who is therefore nothing but treason.[38]

Faced with such frivolous and pompous gibberish, you might question the qualifications of the editors in charge at Gallimard and feel torn between tears, bursts of laughter, and nausea. Over twenty years later, Marty published *The Sex of the Moderns: Neutral Thought and Gender Theory*[39] in which he criticizes in 512 pages Judith Butler's gender theory in the light of Roland Barthes, Gilles Deleuze, Jacques Derrida, Michel Foucault, Jacques Lacan, Claude Lévi-Strauss, Jean-Paul Sartre, and . . . Louis Althusser.

Althusser was therefore the object of many ratiocinations as to his profile and his psychological motivations, including by people who never met him and who were never able to consult his medical file. A similar process was at work in the case of the terrorist who attacked the women at the École Polytechnique de Montréal. Mélissa Blais's work shows that when journalists used psychological expertise to try to explain the event, they legitimized and reinforced the individualist theory while dismissing any sociopolitical reflection on male violence. Writes Blais:

> This type of [psychological] expertise allows journalists to reduce the action [of killing these women] to the singular incident alone . . . and to represent the event as exceptional. Comparisons to other crimes specifically targeting women and analyses pursuing explanations in social relationships are set aside or are overwhelmed by comments . . . in the field of psychology."[40]

Which has the effect of depoliticizing the discussion.

In Althusser's case, the psychological explanation is particularly developed, with the theory of "altruistic suicide" extended by the murderer himself and taken up by commentators.[41] Recounting his hospitalization after the murder and his weekly meetings with his therapist, Althusser writes that he "went over with him over the deep-seated reasons for the murder I had committed, without ever feeling guilty. I remember putting forward a hypothesis . . . Hélène's murder was 'a suicide via a third party'" because she had said that she wanted to die but that she was unable to carry out the act.[42] Althusser had already put forward this thesis in 1982, three years before writing his autobiography:

> I strangled my wife, who meant everything to me, during an intense and unforeseeable state of mental

confusion, in November 1980. She loved me so much, and since she could not go on living, she wanted to die. Unaware of what I was doing and in a state of confusion, I must have "done what she wanted," which she did not resist and which caused her death.[43]

According to this theory, which is astonishing, to say the least, the killer did not murder Hélène Legotien; he committed her suicide out of generosity.[44]

Never short of convoluted explanations to absolve himself of responsibility, Althusser goes on to add:

I was quite clearly seeking *proof*, the counterproof, of *my own objective destruction, the proof of my non-existence*, proof that I was well and truly dead so far as any hope of being saved was concerned . . . But that self-destruction was symbolically achieved through the destruction of others . . . including the woman I loved the most."[45]

Echoing the murderer's words, certain magazines even claimed he was trying to commit suicide: "He strangled her as one commits suicide."[46] These theories in fact function as tactics to hide male violence, pushing the psychologization of the killer even further. The murder is not only legitimized, but Hélène Legotien is no longer a victim. If she still exists in the story, it is the woman who wanted to die and was unable to kill herself. So her murderer did her a favour, he liberated her from her life. She can also simply disappear from the story. In committing this act, Althusser killed himself.

Hélène Legotien no longer exists. She never existed. Only Althusser remains.[47]

In 1992, *Le Monde* published an article about Louis Althusser's madness without once mentioning Hélène Legotien or her murder.[48] On the publication of Althusser's autobiography, this same newspaper questioned "whether it is not the desire for autobiography, that is to say, for existence as the subject of a narrative (in the sense understood by Ricoeur), that acts underground in the murder itself."[49] In short, a great deal of imagination to propose an apparently sophisticated hypotheses, but also a lot of effort to obfuscate a relatively simple fact: whether he was philosopher, a Marxist, or a madman, Althusser was neither more nor less than one of the many men who, every year, kill their spouse or ex-spouse. Such an omission of social phenomena is obtuse to the extreme, given that the killer was the most influential Marxist theoretician of his time. The murder he committed is therefore a social and political matter, regardless of what licensed psychoanalysts, media commentators, and the murderer himself may say. While study after study reveals that the risk of male violence, including murderous violence, increases at moments of separation, commentators rarely acknowledge that Hélène Legotien had threatened to leave her spouse.[50] Whenever it is mentioned, the journalist avoids drawing logical conclusions: "Hélène said she wants to leave him. But also, to die. Did he strangle her to acquiesce her death wish? An impenetrable mystery."[51]

Male Protection and Solidarity

In France, a man with high social capital who assaults a woman, and whose crime is brought to the attention of the public, generally enjoys the protection of considerable friends and allies, who mobilize to defend his honour, absolve him of responsibility for his crime, call for clemency, and criticize feminists. Hélène Legotien's killer was not only a member of the male class, he was also a member of an elevated male caste. Already in nineteenth-century France, excuses were sought and found when the man who murdered his spouse was a banker or a famous writer.[1] In 2013, the editorial in the issue of the journal *Nouvelles Questions féministes* that presented a dossier on "Violence Against Women" noted that "recent media cases of sexual or domestic violence committed by men from the wealthiest backgrounds: the Cantat case,* the Polanski case† or the Strauss-Kahn case‡ have highlighted the complacency of men of these

---

* Singer Bertrand Cantat killed his partner, actress Marie Trintignant, in 2003.

† In 1977, forty-three-year-old film director Roman Polanski drugged and raped a thirteen-year-old girl named Samantha Gailey.

‡ Dominique Strauss-Kahn, then president of the International Monetary Fund, was accused of raping a chambermaid, Ophelia

classes with regard to violence, as well as the solidarity they show to each other."[2]

Sociologist Christine Delphy proposes—regarding public discourse seeking to exonerate and thus protect Dominique Strauss-Kahn, the director of the International Monetary Fund, after a sexual assault on a New York hotel maid—"To consider the incident as an indicator" of what lies in the hearts of the men of the political and intellectual elite in France, a veritable "caste." "They are filled with a misogyny whose depth is equalled only by their class arrogance."[3] This observation is also true when a Marxist philosopher murders his wife.

The murder of Hélène Legotien by her husband confirms these feminist analyses, since the murderer received the support of several male celebrities who came to his defense. Some seem to advocate this type of tactic, such as Bernard-Henri Lévy, who presents himself as a champion of men's rights and oppressed nations but who has also publicly defended Althusser, Cantat, Polanski, and Strauss-Kahn. In fact, in the minutes and hours following the murder, Althusser had the unwavering support of the management of the École normale supérieure, doctors, his friends, and his disciples, who constituted a line of defence even before the judicial authorities took up the case—briefly.

Psychiatrist Michel Dubec notes that "the only exceptional thing in the case is that he did not undergo even an hour of police custody, that is to say that he did

Nafissatou (in addition to sexually assaulting a young journalist, Tristane Banon, and profiting from prostitution rings).

not have the typical trajectory of a mentally ill person who might spend a few hours, or even a few months in prison before being transferred to a psychiatric hospital."[4] Bernard-Henri Lévy, a student of Althusser's, evokes "the conspiracy of the Normaliens, including the author of these lines, who, relying on article 64 of the Penal Code, helped their teacher, who became the first murderer in the history of philosophy, avoid . . . prison."[5]

According to his autobiography, the killer appeared to find this situation rather typical, going so far as to thank the director of the establishment and his friends on several occasions for having manoeuvred so well. He also thanked his teacher, Christian philosopher Jean Guitton, who interrupted "a television programme to declare that he had complete faith in me and would stand by me through thick and thin,"[6] declaring that Althusser was endowed with a "superior intelligence" and "a heart of gold" and that he would be "faithful to him from life to death" (but also affirming, in the same television program in which gay author Yves Navarre participated, that homosexuality "is not in the norm of human nature," equating it to a "a polyp" or "a cancer").[7]

The murderer noted with satisfaction that, "on the whole, the French (and the international) press behaved quite properly, but certain papers really had a field day . . . both wild and malicious," including by denouncing the "scandal that a criminal individual should have been openly protected by the 'establishment': think what would have happened to an ordinary Algerian in the same situation, was the line taken by one 'centrist' newspaper."[8] Indeed, two days after the murder,

Le Quotidien de Paris revealed that a "conspiracy" of Louis Althusser's friends was manoeuvring to "save him from trouble"[9]: "They put him in a car, they drove him to Sainte-Anne's [hospital], they hid him from the very permissive police, from the very slow justice."[10] This disclosure seems unacceptable to the murderer, who speaks as if this protection was due to him, being in the order of things. However, it can be assumed that if "an ordinary Algerian" kills his spouse in France, he will have to face not only the police and the courts but also the public opinion of the majority, which will not see this as an exceptional and inexplicable gesture but rather as further proof of the patriarchal violence of Muslim culture.[11]

Twist to Better Run in Circles

In September 2015, a new collection of Louis Althusser's personal texts was published, under the title *Dreams of Endless Anguish: Dream Stories (1941–1967)* followed by *A Murder Committed by Two*.[1] The book provides readers with the opportunity to explore a series of notes on the murderer's dreams, accompanied by a few pages expounding on his psychoanalyst's suggested interpretations of the murder. This work is not interesting. The dreams are generally insignificant. Althusser is on a train but no longer remembers which city he is travelling to; he's in a store looking for socks before stepping over a torrent with a sword in hand; he's playing tennis with his mother. Others are scabrous; for example, when he has sex with his mother at an orgy. Why then offer the public all this to read? As for the pages relating the psychoanalyst's suggestions, they don't reveal much to anyone who's had the courage to read his autobiography.

This work, written by the famous murderer, demonstrates once more that no effort is spared to disseminate his speech and present him not only as a long-suffering victim but as a genius whose slightest handwritten note might be of public interest. This approach has the effect of totally depoliticizing his crime and of leaving Hélène Legotien in the shadows.

At the heart of the project is a note in which Althusser reports having dreamed that he was killing his sister in 1964, sixteen years before he actually murdered Hélène Legotien. The author of the book's forward, Olivier Corpet, who also worked on the edition of *The Future Lasts a Long Time*, specifies that this note had not been included as an appendix in the autobiography to "avoid hazardous overinterpretations."[2] Such a precaution no longer applies, apparently, twenty years later, not to mention that there was indeed a note on the dream of the sister's murder in the "Materials" section of the appendix of the paperback edition of *The Future Lasts a Long Time*.

In the new book *Dreams of Endless Anguish*, this note is highlighted in a section titled "Premonitory Dreams," a section that contains only two notes. The note becomes an *explanation* for the real murder. And it is not insignificant that the publishers decided to bold the following passage, underlined by the murderer himself in 1984:

> I must kill my sister . . . there is an obligation impossible to avoid, a duty, almost a duty of conscience . . . To kill her with her consent, moreover: a sort of pathetic communion in the sacrifice . . . to give her the death that will save her . . . I am bound to this gift of death . . . to give death as a gift for the other . . . She consents, says yes, it is because she wants it and asks for it, that she knows she must go through it, that I help her.[3]

With such material, anyone can imagine themselves at once psychoanalyst and detective, playing both

Sigmund Freud and Sherlock Holmes simultaneously. It's hard to miss the ultimate clue to explain the 1980 murder, even if this dream, in fact, explains nothing and is unrelated to Hélène Legotien's death. Nonetheless, in his forward, Corpet quotes Althusser, who evoked the "astonishing premonitory appearance" of this dream, which, according to the murderer himself, reveals "the unconscious impulse that led to the tragedy."[4]

It was sold as a scoop, but it was nothing new. The killer had already suggested in his autobiography that murdering his wife could be explained because he wanted to kill his sister, as he'd once dreamed, and also that he'd wanted to kill his psychoanalyst, his father, and his mother. Always dodging social and political interpretation, the editor of *Dreams of Endless Anguish* preferred to employ the thesis of the "a murder committed by two," which is put forward in the note about the psychoanalyst. A theory coupled with the analogy of a sexual relationship:

> Hélène let it happen. I believe that it was a murder committed by two . . . I consider the murder scene to be a scene in which H. must have played an active (even in apparently passive form) and ambiguous role: equivalent to a scene of *sexual seduction*. She must have been active, *provocative* somewhere . . . The murder was carried out by the two of us: it was the realization of *an extreme type of sexual relationship* together. A *folie à deux*.[5]

Indeed, Corpet admits, in passing, that the theory of

"a murder committed by two" "serves too well a desire to *exonerate oneself*" by employing "a theory that is ultimately advantageous" for the murderer.[6] The notion is not further developed.

Rehashing the same story they'd intoned after the publication of Althusser's autobiography, the media covering the release of his latest work once again cast the murderer as a suffering man, a man in crisis, to be pitied. In short, a victim. It is worth noting that the text presenting this theory of the "a murder committed by two" is saturated with references to Althusser's "anguish" (a total of nineteen times in sixteen pages) and to the "suffering," "exhaustion," and "distress" the institutionalized murderer endured. Such language calls its readers to empathize with the murderer.

In *Le Monde des livres*, Élisabeth Roudinesco published a review entitled "Althusser, Reason in Sleep," evoking in its subtitle the "terrifying nightmares" of a philosopher "confronted since 1938 to the tragic experience of melancholy," this "chronically ill patient, twenty times interned and subjected to all possible treatments." Roudinesco's complacent review just reiterates the killer's own account, namely that Hélène Legotien didn't resist her strangulation in any way. As for the murderer, he is "assailed, overwhelmed, afraid" throughout "trying nights" because of his "often terrifying" nightmares. This book would present "a dazzling text" in which the murderer explains that "it is, indeed, he *rightly* says, a '*murder committed by two*' . . . is a kind of *suicidal act*." Roudinesco goes even further, recalling that Jacques Derrida considered that the killer had "condemned" himself by his gesture to be "his own murderer." Finally, the review offers a flight of touching naivety: "It is indeed the author of this *senseless* murder who has best revealed the *truth*."[7]

In the same spirit, a 2015 review in the journal *Les Inrocks* titled "The Dreamlike World of Louis Althusser" by Alexis Pierçon-Gnezda argues that "beyond the often biased and moralizing attempts at interpretation, the work of excavating Althusser's personal archives . . . will have made it possible, finally, to *give the philosopher a voice* to *explain himself* on these facts." It should be understood from these reviews that the speech of a man who killed his spouse is truthful and not biased. According to Pierçon-Gnezda, the public would therefore finally have "the opportunity to understand, through a *movement of empathy*, what Althusser may have experienced and felt in his manic episodes."[8] In *Le Monde diplomatique*, Christophe Baconin sees in this book a "violation" of the murderer's "psychic intimacy," as he'd died twenty-five years previously.[9] Once again, the murderer is the victim.

The introduction for 2015 edition ends with a shocking word. When Corpet is moved by "the singular character of a biographical destiny of a philosopher-murderer, without equivalent in history, which remains fascinating and disconcerting . . . [The destiny] of a major philosopher of our time, [that] of a work that is always present and *alive*."[10]

And yet, a bit of good news. Olivier Corpet announces, in his introduction: "This work is certainly the last in the series of volumes from Louis Althusser's archives."[11]

Lies and Glory

The note presenting the theory of the "a murder committed by two" recalls what had already been emphasized in the autobiography: Hélène Legotien suffered from Althusser's celebrity, which relegated her to a kind of grey zone. According to the murderer, "Death reversed the roles," since he would be "forever the bad one, the *uninteresting case* . . . having endorsed all the critiques [cf. the press], while she [Hélène Legotien] became the poor victim."[1] Like so much of what he's said, the murderer's words ring false.

Althusser remains an icon of Marxist political philosophy; his works continue to be edited and republished; theses,[2] scholarly articles in various languages, and special issues of journals are devoted to him; and there's even a multilingual journal of "Althusserian studies" (*Décalages: An Althusser Studies Journal*). By Olivier Corpet's own admission, "Louis Althusser's work thus experienced an exceptional *posthumous expansion* that saved him from plunging into purgatory."[3] For example, several conferences have celebrated his thought, including Politics and Philosophy in the Works of Louis Althusser in 1991 at the University of Paris-VIII, followed by Althusser Philosopher in 1995 at the Sorbonne and, the same year, Reading Althusser Today, at the scene of the crime, at the École normale supérieure on rue d'Ulm. In 2001, there was the work-shop, About Louis Althusser, of the philosophy section of the Marx International Congress at the University of Paris-Ouest-Nanterre; a day of study, entitled Althusser's Marx in the Political Era of the 1960s, was put on in 2008 by the Centre international d'étude de la philosophie française contemporaine; in 2010 there was About Althusser, which was a collaboration between the Collège international de philosophie and the École nor-male supérieure de Lyon; in 2013 it was For Althusser at the Université Paul-Valéry-Montpellier-III; in 2015, Louis Althusser was organized by the Groupe d'études du materialisme rationnel; also in 2015 was Althusser 1965: The Discovery of the History Continent, again at the scene of the crime, at the École normale supérieure in Paris.

Psychoanalyst and professor at the University of Paris-VII Gérard Pommier has devoted two books to him, *Louis of Nothingness: Althusser's Melancholy* and *Melancholy: Althusser's Life and Works*. The economist Yann Moulier-Boutang authored a two-volume biog-raphy: *Louis Althusser*.

On the cultural scene, the fifty-six-minute docu-mentary film *The Althusser Adventure*, directed by Bruno Oliviero, was broadcast by Arte in 2016. In 2018, the France Culture channel produced an episode entitled "The Althusser Trial" in the series *The Secret Life of Philosophers*, an hour-long interview with the indescribable Éric Marty; and actor Sami Frey read letters from Althusser to Hélène Legotien aloud on the radio in 2019. Two plays have been dedicated to the murder. The first, Antoine Rault's *The Caiman*, a nickname given to the teachers and supervisors of the École normale supérieure, which staged the couple's last night, was performed for several months in 2005 and 2006 at the Théâtre Montparnasse. The newspaper *Le Monde* and even the British daily *The Guardian* reviewed it. And in 2011, Simon Jallade, a former psychiatrist and director of the Saint-Jean-de-Dieu Hospital in Lyon, wrote the play *Althusser's Night*. This work earned Jallade the Journées de Lyon des auteurs de théâtre prize and was selected by the Commission nationale d'Aide à la création de textes dramatiques (Centre national du théâtre). The playwright presents his approach as follows:

> I went to see Althusser. Where he was. In his auto-biography, in his private correspondence. Where he had spoken of himself. Very early on, the idea of a play that would take up this word that had become a dead letter, these words that said so much, took hold. Beyond ideology and clichés, without reopening unnecessary wounds, with respect, it is the Man I wanted to meet.[4]

Three years later, the French Embassy in Beijing awarded the Fu Lei Prize to Cai Hongbin for his translation into Mandarin of *The Future Lasts a Long Time*.

More recently, the Presses universitaires de France published a collection of interviews entitled *Althusser and Us*, edited by Aliocha Wald Lasowski, whose moving portrait opens the introduction:

A philosopher and political thinker, Marxist intellectual, and communist activist, outstanding pedagogue, and editor, Louis Althusser renews and deepens, in an original and innovative way, the political theory and the philosophy of history from Machiavelli to Marx. He has, for over three decades, enthusiastically trained brilliant philosophers . . . Slender and physically strong, the man is passionate about tennis, cycling, and soccer. Discreet and mysterious, with a melancholic face and a cigarette upon his lips, he alternates between lively humour and attentive listening, slipping a smile to his students at the École normale supérieure on rue d'Ulm.[5]

The book consists of some twenty interviews with a handful of intellectuals, including Alain Badiou, Étienne Balibar, Régis Debray, Maurice Godelier, Antonio Negri, Jacques Rancière, and Philippe Sollers, among others. All men. We learn that Michel Foucault had called for readers to "open Althusser's books!" That Jacques Derrida admired "the radiant and provocative force of his thought," and that Roland Barthes considered that "the only acceptable model of science is the one brought to light by Althusser's studies on Marx." Wald Lasowski states that this collection of interviews allows us to measure "the extent to which Althusser's thought remains of burning topicality." Bernard-Henri Lévy, one of the interviewees, testifies that he went to Gordes, where Althusser had acquired a residence in the 1960s, and then shares his anger: "His house is still there. But zero plaques. Zero memorial. And no one, really no one, to remember the monumental master who lived there." It's unlikely that a plaque reminding us that a man who murdered his wife once lived in this building would create a happy atmosphere for its tenants today.

Finally, Althusser's philosophy is also discussed by feminists without any criticism of his murder. In 1990, British philosopher Alison Assiter proposed a book with an intriguing title, *Althusser & Feminism*. It states that "Althusser's theory—considered as a position that stands in itself as a revised version of Marx—is superior to Marx's. It can be considered as such, among other reasons, because it allows us to explain the 'oppression of women' as a phenomenon distinct from class exploitation."[6] That said, the philosopher devotes the first three chapters to discussing Althusserian interpretations of Marxism without mentioning women or feminism, and then two chapters to first criticizing materialist feminists (Christine Delphy, Shulamith Firestone, as well as Mary Daly and Andrea Dworkin) for failing to take into account the biological differences between men and women, in particular with regards to childbirth, as well as Luce Irigaray; all this without mentioning Althusser. The book finally ends with a chapter comparing his theory on ideology and Sigmund Freud's theory on the family, with a long emphasis on the Oedipus complex and penis envy in girls. In 151 pages, there is no (zero) mention of Althusser's wife, Hélène Legotien, or of her murder by the Marxist philosopher.

A few years later, Judith Butler devoted an article to Louis Althusser's concept of "interpellation," titled "Subjugation According to Althusser: 'Conscience Doth

Makes Subjects of Us All,'" in which the "murder of
Hélène, his wife" is mentioned only in passing.[7] The
feminist philosopher specifies that they do not want to
"exploit the biographical element," but nevertheless
devotes a few lines to claiming that Althusser "rushed
into the street to call the police and surrender himself
to justice," with reference to *The Future Lasts a Long
Time*. However, this description of the facts does not
correspond to what can be read in it, since the murderer
explains, rather, that he ran to ask for assistance from the
doctor of the École normale supérieure, whose management saved him from the inquisition of the police and the
courts and saved him from prison. Judith Butler's work
has been widely received, to the point that Éric Marty
notes, in the chapter "The Performative with Althusser"
of his book *The Sex of the Moderns*, that "according
to Butler, Althusser's text [discussed by the feminist],
hitherto forgotten, has found new life by becoming a
classic of the gender corpus."[8]

At least four articles in French and five in English
have been specifically devoted to Butler's piece on
Althusser, including one that appeared in *Actuel Marx*
and was reprinted in English in *Crisis and Critique*,[9] not
to mention those in other languages. Six of these nine
articles do not mention the murder or Hélène Legotien,
including the one published in a feminist academic
journal, signed by Noela Davis, and cited in dozens of
publications.[10] Only one of the nine articles in English
or French touches on the "murder of Hélène," especially
to evoke "the posture of supplicant and tortured later
adopted by someone [Louis Althusser] whom the tragic

circumstances of his personal existence have 'brought to their knees' [as a result of] an irreparable, unforgivable act, which no explanation will ever be able to justify, which is indeed crucifying."[11] Another article remarks on Hélène Rytmann and her murder in passing, and a third mentions the murder, but not the name of the murdered spouse, in a footnote pertaining to theoretical interpretation.[12] Guillaume Le Blanc, who in 2022 coauthored, with Fabienne Brugère, *The World of Women: A Feminist World Tour*, concludes his 2004 article "To Be Subjected: Althusser, Foucault, Butler" with this lyrical flight:

> [The] perception of the intolerable is fundamental to considering new political struggles. Indignation and rage must lead to unprecedented problematizations in the regulated space of knowledge and power. The effects of rage and indignation thus reopen what the analysis of disciplines and the ideological apparatuses of the state [Althusser's famous concept] had too quickly closed by mechanically reducing the subject-function to the subjugation.[13]

It's a shame he neglected to mention the murder of Hélène Legotien, which might indeed provoke "effects of rage and indignation."[14]

Hasana Sharp, a professor at the Institute for Gender, Sexuality, and Feminist Studies at McGill University in Montreal, published "Is it Simple to Be a Feminist in Philosophy? Althusser and Feminist Theoretical Practice" in the journal *Rethinking Marxism*, in 2000, when she was a doctoral student at Pennsylvania State

University.[15] Although she quotes a passage from the autobiography *The Future Lasts a Long Time*, about Karl Marx's comment on Feuerbach's theses that the problem of philosophy should not be to interpret the world but to change it, she manages not to mention the name of Hélène Legotien and not to recall that Althusser killed her.

Can We Separate the Author from His Work?

One of my political science professors at the Université de Montréal said in an amphitheatre sometime around 1985 that we should conclude that Marxism is a failure because, of the two greatest contemporary Marxists, Nicos Poulantzas and Louis Althusser, one died by suicide and the other killed his wife. It was these types of cynical, dishonest comments that provoked a reaction from many Marxists immediately after Althusser murdered Hélène Legotien, who defended a Marxist philosophy whose legitimacy now seemed tainted by his crime. For my part, I have read and reread Althusser's philosophical writings with interest while putting aside the murder of Hélène Legotien. I even have a solid enough grasp of Althusser's philosophy to imagine how some of his theories might explain his marital murder. But such intellectual gymnastics would do him too much honour. I've also read other problematic authors, including Nazis such as Martin Heidegger and Carl Schmitt. I don't, however, dwell on these authors, except when my aim is precisely to grasp the root of their evil, as I did by immersing myself in the hundreds of pages of Althusser's autobiography and again in the hundreds of pages in which the anarchist Pierre-Joseph Proudhon aligns his misogynistic and antifeminist ideas.[1] As for the rest of their work, I am disturbed today by their troubling reminiscences or horrifying images. And I know today that there are literally entire continents of thought that I have never been taught and of which I know little or nothing . . . I am therefore not lacking in reading material; even were I to discard the works written by such men.

For his part, Marxist William S. Lewis, author of *Louis Althusser and the Traditions of French Marxism* and *Concrete Critical Theory: Althusser's Marxism*, wrote an essay in 2019 to justify reading Althusser's philosophical work over and over again, despite, he notes, the fact that it seems to interest very few women philosophers.[2] Responding to recent debates about calls to boycott artists who have raped or killed women, Lewis questions whether it is possible to separate the author from his work; that is, to condemn Althusser's murder while continuing to study and cite his philosophical work. In this very divided debate exists the desire, on the one hand, for the personal satisfaction of reading a text for the sake of freedom. But on the other hand, there is the desire to respect the memory of the victim and to denounce the immunity offered to such aggressors as Althusser. Curiously, this debate often dismisses the anonymous women who have themselves been the target of male violence, or who have witnessed it, or who have heard the testimonies of their sisters or friends, and who remain affected by them. We're talking about millions of women, many of whom are in universities and are active in progressive, communist, and anarchist circles.

I don't know how I'd react, if I were one of them, to the publication of a new book by Althusser or to the announcement of a new lecture devoted to his philosophy. I can imagine that it probably wouldn't be my priority to devote time and energy to it and that I might feel uncomfortable, pained, hurt, humiliated, concerned, betrayed, angry.

In the spring of 2023 at the École normale supérieure in Paris, graffiti appeared above the door of a seminar room known as the Raymond Aron room: "The Hélène Legotien-Rytmann room: resistance fighter and sociologist victim of femicide in 1980 at the ENS." And on the door, a plaque inscribed with the words: "In memory of Hélène Legotien-Rytmann, sociologist and resistance fighter murdered by her husband [L. Althusser] in 1980 at the ENS. We don't forget. We don't forgive."[3]

I don't know who graffitied the space, but I imagine that it is certainly more politically and even philosophically stimulating for many women abused by men than all of Althusser's intellectual work—not to mention his filthy autobiography and the many studies of it—if we accept William S. Lewis's own definition of political philosophy: "To create, analyze, and propose true or adequate ideas about how one should live with others."[4]

Conclusion

What do we know about Hélène Legotien today? Almost nothing, except that she was murdered by her illustrious husband. She's ultimately died twice, and her murderer is responsible for both of her deaths. He killed her first with his own hands and then a second time by occupying the entire public space to talk about himself under the pretense of addressing her death. A quick web search (with Google) leads me to see that there is almost no information available about her. Searching for her, in fact, almost inevitably leads us instead to her killer, Althusser.

This murdered woman nevertheless participated in sociological research on labour[1] and published essays in the journal *Esprit*, among others, under her resistance name: Hélène Legotien (see her bibliography at the end of the book). She reviewed the film *We Are All Assassins*, released in 1952. She noted, of the production, that "the sex, banditry, and *crime of passion* . . . have complete freedom to express themselves. We know to what mediocrity these themes condemn most Western films."[2]

Hélène Legotien lived in her husband's shadow, where she still lingers, even after the death of her murderer. In 1985, the journalist, novelist, and essayist Claude Sarraute wrote in *Le Monde*: "We in the media, as soon as we see a prestigious name involved in a juicy trial, Althusser, Thibault d'Orléans,[3] we make a big deal out of it. The victim? They don't even get three lines. The culprit is the star."[4] Vania Widmer confirms this statement: "I can't find Hélène Rytmann's voice in any of my readings. She too, it can be said, was killed twice."[5] It was, however, following the publication of Sarraute's text that the murderer was encouraged by his friends to write his autobiography. In a personal letter, he explicitly referred to this "article by C. Sarraute in *Le Monde*" whose terms he had "hardly appreciated" and he deplored his "crude thesis . . . according to which in these 'juicy' cases we are only interested in the culprit, and not in the victim."[6] He specifies that he gathered documentation to tear this thesis to pieces, including an article in the journal *Perspectives psychiatriques*, which presents two profiles with which he identifies: (1) "acute psychopathological states" and (2) "delusions of persecution with self-legitimization of the homicidal idea."[7]

Widmer thus notes that when Sarraute "notices that Hélène Althusser is not being talked about enough, then Louis Althusser begins to talk about himself."[8]

A few women are making efforts to celebrate the memory of Hélène Legotien. Sylvie Germain wrote the prose poem "Pour Hélène" inspired by a photo taken in 1951 near Le Brusc, in the Var, in which it is difficult to distinguish the frail body of Hélène Legotien from the trees. In 2022, historian Lucie Rondeau du Noyer published an article on the *Mediapart* website called "The Courage of Hélène Legotien." She recalls that Hélène Legotien was an employee of the Society for Economic and Social Development Studies (SÉDÉS) until her retirement and that she participated as a sociologist in the writing of studies mainly devoted to the rural development of France and its former colonies in Africa . . . These scientific articles are co-authored with agronomists or professionals higher up in the hierarchy of the SÉDÉS. In 1979 and 1980, she conducted a voluntary survey on the family life of French workers. By scrupulously collecting their words, she hoped to understand the persistence of their malaise and exploitation, despite the three decades of high growth that France had just gone through since 1945. When her husband's deteriorating mental health allowed her, Legotien went to investigate in Port-de-Bouc with the support of the communist town hall and the complicity of a team of local researchers. In 1984, this group of researchers published a report entitled "From the shipyard to the factory: the workers' memory of Port-de-Bouc."

This report is dedicated to the memory of Hélène Legotien. Rondeau du Noyer has also proposed a bibliography of her writings (reproduced at the end of this little book).

For a man, says male violence expert Jalna Hanmer, "it may be or appear necessary to kill, maim, incapacitate, or temporarily compromise a woman's ability to provide services to remain the master. Prestige, respect, self-esteem: this is what a man earns, expresses, and makes recognized through the appropriation of others."[9] Most certainly, Hélène Legotien's killer knew how to manipulate the murder itself to rework his prestige, respect, and self-esteem, and his friends and accomplices also devoted a great deal of time and energy towards this task, with the support of esteemed institutions (universities, newspapers, publishing houses). This, again, is a social phenomenon.

Clearly, the murder of Hélène Legotien was not an exceptional event; Louis Althusser was banal, just another woman killer.

Epilogue: The Spectre of Hélène Legotien

Writing nearly forty years after a murder in November 1980, I naively believed that this "matter" belonged to history, to the past, to the world of the dead rather than of the living.[1] The femicide took place at a time when the term itself was not yet well known. It dated from the "last century," as they say, from the distant era of the Cold War and the USSR. The murderer was a Marxist philosopher the likes of whom we no longer see.

And yet. The French edition of this little book arrived in bookstores in France on September 8, 2023, and *the next day*, I got a message about it, sent to my email address at the Université du Québec à Montréal (UQAM). The message opened as follows: "Hello Mr. Dupuis-Déri, I am writing you this email because I am a student at the ENS Ulm," the institution where Hélène Legotien was murdered nearly forty-three years ago, "and I have just read your book." It is true that it is a short book and a quick read. The student, Clarisse Gruyters, whom I did not know, informed me that she was "part of the group of feminist activists at the ENS who'd installed the commemorative plaque for Hélène Légotien-Rytmann," of which a photo is included at the beginning of the book. Already very moved by her story, I was overwhelmed when I read: "I also wanted to inform you that this plaque, made in early 2023, was, unfortunately, vandalized, alongside the entire room, by masculinist graffiti," such as "Down with feminists!," "in the wake of the events of March 23 when masculinist neo-Nazis, the 'waffen assas,' attacked the ENS demonstration procession" during the pension reform protests. A quick search online allowed me to learn about this group, Waffen ASSAS, a terrible play on words in reference to the Waffen SS—the SS squadrons of the Nazi regime—which became Waffen Assas, from the name of the Université de Paris Pathéon-Assas, known for its right-wing and far-right student organizations.

In the National Assembly, a deputy from France Insoumise even referred to these events explicitly, stating that "the militants of the Groupe union défense (GUD), recently reformed after five years of absence, are clearly hiding behind the 'Waffen Assas.'" These attacks would certainly have outraged resistance fighter Hélène Legotien, but she would not have been surprised that the far-right was so antifeminist: fascism and Nazism have historically been built, among other things, on the myth of the feminization of societies and institutions, to which a (re)virilization of the men of the nation must respond. The far-right leader Éric Zemmour says much the same in his pamphlet *The First Sex*. In her email, Gruyters added that the plaque, removed for cleaning, was then misplaced, but there was a project to reinstall it. The ENS student also confided that discussing the femicide perpetrated by Althusser is not an easy task because . . . there are still many events organized to promote his thought, but the change of name of the Aron room to the Legotien room was very fluid for all the students [and] this room is now recognized as the Legotien room. In addition, I wanted to mention the virtual non-existence of courses at the ENS on subjects such as gender, gender violence, feminist issues, etc. And when they exist, they are very, very limited, and discuss "women" more than gender issues.

She concluded her correspondence by disclosing that when, in the context of her master's degree in theory and analysis of law, she speaks up in class about her research on gender violence and the legal categorization of femicides, she is made to understand that these themes are not scientific "and that they are not interesting for law, or even for philosophy. It would only be a question of a social and militant fight." Discouraging.

A few days later, on October 1, 2023, another email arrived from France, entitled "Thank you for Hélène," from feminist historian Mathilde Larrère of the Université de Paris-Est Marne-la-Vallée, who authored, among others, *Rage Against the Machismo*.[2] She wrote:

Hélène was a good friend of my father, Raphael Larrère [an agronomist specializing in environmental ethics]. I remember his tears when she died, his anger against Althusser. I also remember how disgusted my parents were when he escaped judgment, when he was released. A woman—their friend—had been

murdered, and it was like nothing had happened. I
read the murderer's memoirs through this perspective,
and my father told me, "Don't let yourself be fooled
by his justifications."

On the same day, I received another message, entitled
"Althusser Book," this time from Jo Ros, an author from
the south of France whom I knew no more than Gruyters
and Larrère. He also shared a testimony with me:

> In the 1980s, as Director of the Municipal Cultural
> Office of the city of Port-de-Bouc, a port in the south
> of France [where Hélène Legotien conducted socio-
> logical research], I led with the works councils of the
> Fos industrial zone and a collective of creators and
> scientists, the workers' memory of the shipyard that
> the city lost in 1966, wounding an entire population
> and the starting point for the industrial memories of
> closed factories . . . Unexpectedly, after listening to a
> program on France Culture, Hélène Legotien wants to
> meet me at all costs . . . and ends up showing up in my
> office (with the enthusiasm you can guess) and imposes
> her participation at her own expense in the work of
> the scientists of the collective set up. She makes her
> contribution by innovating a method: to *immediately
> return what she learns from her investigations to the
> workers without waiting for a publication, during
> the "Rendez-vous de la mémoire."* [Emphasis in the
> original.] So she follows this action at my side, not
> without an anguish and anxiety towards Louis, who
> is not doing very well at that time. I will skip over

the details (phone call from the philosopher at my home, long discussion with my wife, with myself, on the work shared with Hélène, etc.). The couple's stay in the city under the seal of secrecy.

This touching message ended like a sledgehammer: "Finally, on her last trip to meet with the collective, on Sunday, November 15 [1980], we spent the day together. I accompanied her on the night train and learned of the tragedy on the radio early the next morning." Thus, what the murderer explains to us in his autobiography, and which I myself reported, is not entirely accurate: the couple was not isolated in the weeks and days preceding the tragedy, since Hélène was carrying out her own activities far from Paris. But Althusser seemed to be irritated by this.

In addition to replying to these messages, I forwarded them to my editor, who, like me, saw the formation of a small affinity community in memory of Hélène Legotien.

In early November, I received a new message entitled "Féminicide," signed by the novelist Marie Darrieussecq, with whom I had never been in touch. She explained to me that her reading of Althusser's letters to Hélène Legotien and his "unbearable" autobiography had "turned my stomach, my heart, my brain for far too long." Teaching French as a foreign language at the ENS, she said that "once a week" she walks "in front of the cardboard that has replaced the graffiti in memory of Ms. Rytmann Legotien. While the cardboard is sometimes torn off, it is always replaced. And I found your book in an extraordinary place . . . An extraordinary day . . . I'm running out of time, but I'll tell you about it."

Shortly thereafter, she found the time, and wrote:

I am leading a writing workshop in a branch of a psychiatric hospital . . . at the Bibliothèque du Pôle Paris Centre, one of the last places that maintains the legacy of Jean Oury [psychiatrist and psychoanalyst], along with the Péniche l'Adamant and a few others, who send psychotic adults interested in writing there. And why was I thinking of Althusser that Tuesday? I had just returned from the Basque Country, where I spend almost half of my time, and I had taken from my bookcase these two large bricks (his letters and his [autobiographical] book), with the idea of putting them in the recycling bin, to free up some space. But then I felt remorseful. I was planning to read them again one day to make sure that the anger I felt just touching them was well founded. I boarded my train without acting. And *there*, on the big table around which we gather to write, *there*, in the library, your little green book (small but mighty). It was the only book off the shelves. With this title: *Althusser Assassin*. While the passengers of the Adamant were working (the order of the day was: "A genie comes out of a bottle, what do you ask of him, as a wish?"), I started reading it. Around the big table, there is the one that all the books talk about, there is the one who is watched by God (unlike neurotics, he *knows* that God is watching him), there is the music madman, there is the one who is so agitated that writing, sitting at this table, is a brief fixed point to which he can stand for an hour and it relaxes him. And the others, and I [immersed in reading] your book. That's the story. Have a good Sunday.

I also received a new message from historian Mathilde Larrère, whose father had been a friend of Hélène Logitien's, who wrote to me this time about the Sévriennes, a nickname designating the students of the École normale supérieure de jeunes filles de Sèvres, which dissolved in 1985 and then merged with the ENS in the rue d'Ulm: "My mother had bad memories of Althusser, a teacher in Ulm, who did not want the Sévriennes (when the ENS was not mixed) to attend his classes, women, you know, bothered the guy." Thus, this Marxist philosopher rejected female students on the basis of their gender! No wonder his young disciples were only men, a true *boys' club*.

I received other messages, including from Quebec, from feminist academics and activists who wanted to share with me their memories of the 1970s and 1980s, of the domineering Marxism in their political networks in France, of the murder that made so few waves at the time, of the wife of a famous Marxist theorist.

Johanna Luyssen, a journalist from the French newspaper *Libération* then became interested in the subject and wrote a long article in December 2023. Ros specifies, with regards to Hélène Legotien's visits to Port-de-Bouc, that "Althusser often called. It was as if he was tracking her. He constantly wanted to know where she was, what she was doing. Hélène often slept at the house of my wife Alice and I, so he called home." These are all typical behaviours of a violent man exercising coercive control over his partner. Another sad banality. Hélène Legotien then confided in them that her husband was violent and that she was apprehensive about her return to Paris.

The *Libération* journalist commented the following: "The typical mechanisms of femicide were there, clearly visible. In addition to his recurrent desire to control his wife's activities, Louis Althusser made her suffer a great deal." She also quotes the academic specialist in male violence Pauline Delage: "When the aggressor is of the upper class, or white, his violence is more psychologized. This is not the case for the working or non-white classes. However, Louis Althusser is part of the elite." The *Libération* article *finally* recalls that the murderer died of a heart attack in 1990, after living in a Parisian apartment that Hélène Legotien had acquired "in anticipation of retirement."[3] Columnist Dov Alfon notes that "a plaque [in memory of Hélène Legotien] at the entrance to the École normale supérieure would be the least we could do."

In the winter of 2024, a French academic wrote to me and asked to speak to me personally. François Picard Rader, professor emeritus of ethnomusicology at the Sorbonne, wanted to explain to me that an inheritance had enabled him to buy a home in Belleville in March 1980. The transaction had been somewhat arduous, as the real estate agent required him to wait for the decision of another potential buyer, a certain professor named *Albuther* or *Althuber*. It was obviously Althusser, who phoned or sent a new fax every day to the real estate agent, asking for an extension of the deadlines. His problem? Married, he needed his wife's permission to take out a loan and determine the choice of family home. However, it was not to move there with her, according to the real estate agent, but rather to house a pregnant lover! Did the real estate agent report the facts? Did this woman finally have the child? Who knows. But all this took place barely eight months before the philosopher killed Hélène Legotien, who was, by her own admission, trying to leave him.

———————

Of all the books I have published, I have never received such feedback, such testimonials, such engagement. While the influx has since slowed, I did receive a message from the historian Lucie Rondeau du Noyer on November 21, 2024, more than a year after the original publication of the book. I had already corresponded with the woman to whom we owe a bibliographical work retracing the work of Hélène Legotien and who has begun to publish the results of her research on Legotien.[4] Now, she shared some excellent news with me:

> A plaque in memory of Hélène Legotien Rytmann will be unveiled on Monday, November 25, at the ENS de Paris and in the medium term, it is intended to take place in a "space" of the École whose exact location I do not yet know . . . I am currently carrying out a mission to evaluate and collect the archives, which may lead to the creation of a collection of Hélène Legotien's personal archives (and separate from her

husband's collection!) [including the letters addressed to him, which rumour claimed were lost forever]. From an institutional perspective, 2024 is therefore a turning point in the treatment of Legotien's legacy.

She also attached the speech she gave on this occasion and a photo of the plaque. In this speech, the historian clears up several misunderstandings about Hélène Legotien:

> During the three decades that she was linked to Althusser, Legotien was . . . far from having formed a fusional couple with him and also far from having been confined to reproductive and care activities within the walls of 45 rue d'Ulm . . . Hélène Legotien has not always lived in the shadow of her partner. In 1950, [she] was much better known (for better or for worse) in Parisian communist circles than her young companion . . . Legotien was not despised, [and] her texts were read and discussed in the same way as those of other authors.

She added that "it is also possible to demonstrate that some of the philosopher's theoretical and political texts were influenced by the militant trajectory and sociological work of his companion." This last remark echoes the magnificent work of Valérie Lefebvre-Faucher, presented in *Jenny, Eleanor, and Laura, et al: This Is Not a Book About Marx*, which explains how Karl Marx's wife and daughters, all intellectuals and socialist activists, clearly inspired his work:

An entire family bore the name Marx. A joyful, supportive, funny, and idealistic clan of Marxes, who were passionate about literature and defying every authority. A gang of feminists. Why do we persist in upholding this image of the great man alone in his frame? . . . Why don't we talk about the clan, about the collective action of thinking? Is it less serious because the whole family was involved?[5]

Similarly, Hélène Legotien is said to have influenced the ideas of her murderer of a spouse, which would not be surprising since she was also a communist, researcher, and author.

Lucie Rondeau du Noyer sent me a photograph of the plaque, on which we can read that she identifies a "space dedicated to Hélène Rytmann":

The daughter of Jewish merchants from the Russian Empire, Hélène Rytmann took a degree in history and, from 1932, was an active member of the Communist Party. Between 1935 and the beginning of the Second World War, she carried out her professional and trade union activities in the world of cinema . . . From 1951, Hélène Legotien trained in sociology . . . first as an employee of the OEEC [Organisation for European Economic Cooperation] and then as a field investigator on behalf of Alain Touraine and Pierre Naville. At the end of 1963, she became a full-time research fellow at the Société d'études pour le développement économique et social. Built around long interviews with farmers and workers, her sociological studies of urban and rural development inspired many of her economist and agronomist colleagues.

The murderer had chosen to title his autobiography, written to justify his murder, *The Future Lasts a Long Time*. When you think about it, these are probably the only relevant words in this abominable cobblestone.

––––––––––

Among all these messages received, one of them invited itself into my mailbox with a very intriguing title: "Althusser and Feminism." It was sent to me by my colleague, comrade, and friend Michel Lacroix, a professor of literature who is very knowledgeable about Marxism,[6] who was then in Paris. He wanted to present me with his "little find of the day, in the Althusser archives. A violently anti-feminist text [with] a very muddy background." Attached was the transcription of the nine-page document, typewritten annotated as "proofs" and catalogued without date.[7]

The future murderer of Hélène Legotien, whom I naively believed to be ignorant or disinterested in the feminism of his time, explains himself on this subject as follows, in a commentary on his own—insignificant— text "On Conjugal Obscenity" from 1951[8]:

"Feminism" is above all an ideology which, declaring itself for the "liberation of women," finds the essence of its means in the theoretical and practical denunciation of Man as enemy number 1, the "machismo," the "phallic," the holder of "power" in itself, in short the "secular responsible" for the servitude (if not the exploitation!) of "Woman" . . . which is now beginning to take its historical revenge . . . The systematic "hatred" of man, of the male sex, goes so far as to provoke the physical and social separation of certain groups of women . . . in the rejection of the heterosexual act, in the constitution of "Communities of Women" . . . groups of women give themselves up to female homosexuality, not out of desire, but out of political conviction, and even accept the idea of artificial fertilization . . . The Man is treated as enemy number 1.

Thus, Louis Althusser lamented that the feminists of his time could criticize men and even be lesbians! Poor man. And this future murderer continues, taking a path—and a voice—so revealing:

It is enough to put forward the hypothesis that a masculinist ideology would be constituted (why not, in principle?) that would denounce "the exploitation and secular oppression that Woman" imposes on Man . . . This masculinist (and not "macho") ideology would have no trouble discussing the role of the woman from pregnancy to childbirth . . . the decisive role of the mother for most of the vital and psychic functions of the child or even of the adolescent, if not of adulthood (how many men have no other "desire" than to fulfill that of "their mother"?) and of all the advantages which, rightly or wrongly, are attributed to her in civilian life (the majority of women still remain at home today; no military service . . .). The list is long, and if we had to evoke all the fantasies of the "devouring mother" who, under the functions of the "mother of the family" consecrated in all Christian countries . . . or of the "housewife," haunts the existence of many men, and literally "prevents them from living," because these fantasies are only the variation of the terrible complex of "castration" (or of the extreme weakness and vulnerability of the man's sex), against which man or Man tries in vain to defend himself by the well-known parades of over-mastering his powerlessness.

The famous Marxist philosopher, adulated even by feminists, had already, long before killing his wife, developed a sharp critique of feminism, and even anticipated the arguments of the *masculinist*, misogynistic, and antifeminist movement, for which men are dominated by women, including their "all-consuming" mothers and "castrating" feminists.[9]

Today, we know well what such victimhood resentment can justify, in terms of murderous violence.

Hélène Legotien's Bibliography

Bibliography compiled with the help of Lucie Rondeau du Noyer's essay, "Le courage d'Hélène Legotien," *Mediapart*, 16 November 2022.

Film Criticism

"Camarade P," *Combat*, 22 November 1944, 2.

"*L'Air de Paris* de Marcel Carné," *Esprit*, January 1955, 135–38.

"Du roman au film," *Esprit*, July 1955, 1144–64.

"*Le Chant des fleuves* de Joris Ivens," *Esprit*, July 1955, 1186–89.

"*Le Chant des fleuves* de Joris Ivens" (excerpts), in *Joris Ivens*, ed. Abraham Zalzman (Paris: Seghers, 1963), 166ff.

Sociology Studies

"Propositions pour une réorganisation des actions de développement rural," *Développement et civilisations*, no. 38 (June 1969): 24–38 (coauthors: Gilbert Ancian and Bernard Manlhiot).

"Cultures d'exportation ou cultures vivrières," *Rythmes du Monde* 43, nos. 3–4 (1969) (coauthors: Gilbert Ancian and Bernard Manlhiot).

"Les méthodes d'enquête par sondage en milieu rural africain," *Techniques et développement*, no. 8 (July–August 1973): 16–21 (coauthor: Henri Raymond).

Unpublished Sociology Studies

"Note de méthode sur une activité sociologique à la SÉDÉS," Paris, Secteur Recherche de la SÉDÉS, February 1964.

"La planification interrégionale dans l'agriculture: les obstacles à l'évolution des systèmes de production," Paris, SÉDÉS/Délégation générale à la recherche scientifique et technique, October 1967, vol. 2.

"Représentation du Mirail auprès des ménages et des promoteurs toulousains," Société d'équipement de la Haute-Garonne et de l'Ariège/Centre d'études et de recherches sur l'aménagement urbain, 1968 (coauthor: Édouard Kleinmann).

"Les résultats qualitatifs de l'enseignement dans les États de l'Afrique Noire francophone," Problèmes de l'aide à l'éducation dans le Tiers Monde, Paris, section française de l'Association internationale pour le développement, 1970, 59–117.

"Sur les structures internes et externes de l'économie agricole traditionnelle africaine," Paris, SÉDÉS, October–November 1971.

"Étude méthodologique générale sur les structures propres au développement rural et régional: enquête de base au niveau des villages (identification des villages, recherche des indicateurs, questionnaires, méthode de stratification et exemple d'application)," Paris, SÉDÉS/ Secrétariat d'État aux Affaires étrangères chargé de la Coopération, March 1974 (coauthors: G. Cancelier et Henri Raymond).

"Les problèmes agricoles déclenchés par la création d'une autoroute en rase campagne," Scetauroute/ SÉDÉS, September 1975.

"Étude sociologique," n.d. (coauthor: M. Moiroud).

Hélène Legotien was also a contributing editor to:

"L'approvisionnement des villes dans les pays franco-phones d'Afrique et de Madagascar: enquêtes et perspectives," Paris, SÉDÉS/SEAE (Secrétariat d'État aux Affaires étrangères chargé de la Coopération), December 1972.

Acknowledgements

This text reproduces in a revised form two articles published in the journal *Nouvelles Questions féministes*: "La banalité du mâle: Louis Althusser a tué sa conjointe, Hélène Rytmann-Legotien, qui voulait le quitter" (The banality of the male: Louis Althusser killed his spouse, Hélène Rytmann-Legotien, who wanted to leave him), 34, no. 1 (2015) 84–101 and "Postscript de l'article 'La banalité du mâle: Louis Althusser a tué sa conjointe, Hélène Rytmann-Legotien, qui voulait le quitter'" (Postscript of the article 'The banality of the male: Louis Althusser killed his spouse, Hélène Rytmann-Legotien, who wanted to leave him') 35, no. 1 (2016) 131–5. I would like to thank *Nouvelles Questions féministes* for the authorization to reproduce both texts here. I would also like to thank Omer Moussaly for his research and Rachel Bédard, Christine Delphy, Anne Migner-Laurin, Geneviève Pagé, Patricia Roux, and an anonymous NQF evaluator for their insightful recommendations. I would also like to thank Éditions du remue-ménage for their renewed confidence, and all the other individuals—especially women—who participated in the production of this book. I cannot emphasize enough that my feminist reflections, including on the subject of male violence, owe so much to sociologist Mélissa Blais, a specialist on the matter.

—FDD, Montreal, 5 June 2023

Notes

Introduction

1. Louis Althusser, *The Future Lasts a Long Time: Genius, Madness, and Murder—The Extraordinary Autobiography of France's Greatest Modern Thinker,* trans. Veasey Richard (New York: Vintage, 1994), 228; but this account has been debated by Éric Marty in *Louis Althusser, un sujet sans procès: anatomie d'un passé très récent* (Paris: Gallimard, 1999), 192.

2. Althusser, *Future Lasts a Long Time,* 275.

3. Louis Althusser, *Écrits philosophiques et politiques*, vol. 1 (Paris: Stock/IMEC, 1994), 535. See also "Trois experts psychiatres examineront M. Louis Althusser," *Le Monde*, 20 November 1980.

4. C.B., "Le magistrat instructeur n'a pas pu notifier son inculpation d'homicide à M. Louis Althusser: meurtre et psychopathologie," *Le Monde*, 19 November 1980.

5. Christine Delphy, "C'est le plus grand des voleurs, oui mais c'est un Gentleman," in *Un troussage de domestique* (Paris: Syllepse, 2011), 7.

6. Patrizia Romito, *Un silence de mortes: la violence masculine occultée* (Paris: Syllepse, 2006), 155.

Feminist Insights

1. Pauline Delage, Delphine Lacombe, Marylène Lieber, Solenne Jouanneau, Magali Mazuy, "De la violence létale contre les femmes à la violence féminicide: genèse et mobilisations," *Cahiers;* see camillegharbi.com/actsoflove.

2. Ghislaine Guérard and Anne Lavender, "Le fémicide conjugal, un phénomène ignoré: analyse de la couverture journalistique de trois quotidiens montréalais," *Recherches féministes*, 12, no. 2 (1999): 159–77.

3. Annik Houel, Patricia Mercader, and Helga Sobota, *Crime passionnel, crime ordinaire*, (Paris: Presses universitaires de France, 2003), 9, 103ff.

4. The same double standard can be observed in media accounts of terrorist attacks in North America and Europe.

5. Marylène Lieber, *Genre, violences et espaces publics: la vulnérabilité des femmes en question* (Paris: Presses de Sciences Po, 2008), 175.

6. Houel, Mercader, and Sobota, *Crime passionnel*, 104–5.

7. While the text of Blais's book has been translated from the French, the book is available in English: Mélissa Blais, "'I Hate Feminists!': December 6, 1989, and Its Aftermath (Halifax, NS: Fernwood Publishing, 2014); Patrizia Romito, *Un silence de mortes: la violence masculine occultée* (Paris: Syllepse, 2006).

8. For an analysis of the École Polytechnique massacre as an anti-feminist terrorist attack, see also Mélissa Blais, Francis Dupuis-Déri, Lyne Kurtzman, and Dominique Payette (eds.), *Retour sur un attentat antiféministe: École polytechnique de Montréal, 6 décembre 1989* (Montreal, Remue-ménage, 2010).

9. Patrizia Romito, *Un silence de mortes*, 137; see also Jalna Hanmer, "Violence et contrôle social des femmes," *Questions féministes*, no. 1 (1977).

10. Patrizia Romito, *Un silence de mortes,* 122–23.

11. Mélissa Blais, "Masculinist Discourses on Intimate Partner Violence: Antifeminist Men Defending White Heterosexual Male Supremacy," in *Men, Masculinities and Intimate Partner Violence*, eds. Lucas Gottzén, Margunn Bjørnholt, and Floretta Boonzaier (London: Routledge, 2021), 81–96. See also by the same author, "Effets des tactiques antiféministes auprès des institutions œuvrant contre les violences faites aux femmes,"

in *Antiféminismes et masculinismes d'hier et d'aujourd'hui,* eds. Christine Bard, Mélissa Blais, and Francis Dupuis-Déri (Paris: Presses universitaires de France, 2019), 437–62 and "Masculinisme et violences contre les femmes: une analyse des effets du contremouvement antiféministe sur le mouvement féministe québécois" (PhD diss., Université du Québec à Montréal, 2018).

12. Mélissa Blais, "'I Hate Feminists!'" 77ff. Note that this is a question of media discourse on femicide, while feminists have also developed psychological analyses of violence against women. See Stéphanie Pache, "L'histoire féministe de la 'psychologisation des violences,'" *Cahiers du genre,* no. 66 (2019): 51–70.

13. Hanmer, "Violence et contrôle."

The Social Context of the Murder

1. Louis Althusser, *The Future Lasts a Long Time: Genius, Madness, and Murder—The Extraordinary Autobiography of France's Greatest Modern Thinker,* trans. Veasey Richard (New York: Vintage, 1994), 16.

2. Vania Widmer, "Le crime d'Althusser," *L'Écrit,* no. 54 (2004): 13; see also Catherine A. Poisson, "Louis Althusser's The Future Lasts a Long Time: The Failure of Auto-Redemption," *Journal of Twentieth-Century/Contemporary French Studies* 2, no. 1 (1998): 107–25.

3. Annik Houel, Patricia Mercader, and Helga Sobota, *Crime passionnel, crime ordinaire* (Paris: Presses universitaires de France, 2003), 129.

4. "L'autopsie conclut à un décès par strangulation," *Le Monde,* 18 November 1980.

5. Pauline Delage, *Violences conjugales: du combat féministe à la cause publique* (Paris: Presses de Sciences Po, 2017); Maryse Jaspard, *Les violences contre les femmes* (Paris: La Découverte, 2005), 11–13; Alice Debauche and Christelle

Hamel, "Violence des hommes contre les femmes: quelles avancées dans la production des savoirs?," *Nouvelles Questions féministes* 32, no. 1 (2013), 5.

6.   Jalna Hanmer, "Violence et contrôle social des femmes," *Questions féministes*, no. 1 (1977).

7.   Carol Hanisch, "The Personal Is Political (1970)," in *Radical Feminism: A Documentary Reader,* ed. Barbara A. Crow (New York: New York University Press, 2000), 113–16.

8.   Geraldine Finn, *Why Althusser Killed His Wife: Essays on Discourse and Violence, Atlantic Highlands* (Humanities Press, 1996), 5–7.

9.   Althusser, *Future Lasts a Long Time*, 145.

10.   Julie Lefebvre and Suzanne Léveillée, "Profil descriptif d'hommes ayant commis un homicide conjugal au Québec," in *Le passage à l'acte dans la famille: perspectives psychologique et sociale*, eds. Suzanne Léveillée and Julie Lefebvre (Québec: Presses de l'Université du Québec, 2011), 12.

11.   Althusser, *Future Lasts a Long Time*, 251.

12.   Althusser, *Future Lasts a Long Time*, 251.

13.   Lefebvre and Léveillée, "Profil descriptif d'hommes," 12.

14.   Althusser, *Future Lasts a Long Time*, 243.

15.   Althusser, *Future Lasts a Long Time*, 248.

Psychologization and Victimization

1.   Olivier Corpet and Yann Moulier-Boutang, foreword to *L'avenir dure longtemps*, by Louis Althusser (Paris: Stock/IMEC, 1994), 18.

2.   Corpet and Moulier-Boutang, foreword; Louis Althusser, *Lettres à Hélène* (Paris: Grasset/IMEC, 2011), 59; Marc Chabot, "L'avenir dure longtemps de Louis d'Althusser: les récits d'un échec de la pensée . . . où abondent les vérités," *Le Soleil*, 29 June 1992, A9.

3.   Bernard-Henri Lévy, preface to *Lettres à Hélène*, by Louis Althusser, 8.

4. Louis Althusser, *The Future Lasts a Long Time: Genius, Madness, and Murder—The Extraordinary Autobiography of France's Greatest Modern Thinker,* trans. Veasey Richard (New York: Vintage, 1994), 31.

5. Althusser, *Future Lasts a Long Time,* 116.

6. Althusser, *Future Lasts a Long Time,* 170, emphasis in the original.

7. Althusser, *Future Lasts a Long Time,* 171.

8. Althusser, *Future Lasts a Long Time,* 55–63.

9. Althusser, *Future Lasts a Long Time,* 36.

10. Althusser, *Future Lasts a Long Time,* 56.

11. Althusser, *Future Lasts a Long Time,* 132, emphasis in the original.

12. Althusser, *Future Lasts a Long Time,* 165.

13. Althusser, *Future Lasts a Long Time,* 215, 226.

14. Althusser, *Future Lasts a Long Time,* 225.

15. Althusser, *Future Lasts a Long Time,* 106, emphasis in the original.

16. Althusser, *Future Lasts a Long Time,* 106.

17. Althusser, *Future Lasts a Long Time,* 52.

18. Althusser, *Future Lasts a Long Time,* 88.

19. Althusser, *Future Lasts a Long Time,* 28.

20. He uses this image three times in two pages.

21. Althusser, *Future Lasts a Long Time,* 28.

22. Vania Widmer, "Le crime d'Althusser," *L'Écrit,* no. 54 (2004): 11.

23. Michel Contat, "Les morts d'Althusser," *Le Monde,* 24 April 1992, 25; Philippe Chevallier, "Hélène et Louis," *L'Express,* no. 3124, 18 May 2011, 116; Martine de Rabaudy, "Le fou de Franca," *L'Express,* no. 2472, 19 November 1998, 134.

24. Valérie Marin La Meslée, "'Deux morts' de Louis Althusser," *Magazine littéraire,* no. 458 (2006): 96.

25. Chevallier, "Hélène et Louis."

26. Lévy, preface, 11, emphasis added.

27. "Althusser, le lyrisme et la déraison," *Le Monde,* 26 May 2011.

In 2021, Jean Birnbaum wrote an essay on the subject of public debates entitled *Le courage de la nuance* (Seuil).

28. Lucile Cipriani, "Mort de Marie Trintignant: nul n'a su contourner l'agresseur," *Le Devoir*, 3 September 2003.

29. Maryse Jaspard, *Les violences contre les femmes* (Paris: La Découverte, 2005), 111.

30. Dominique Dhombres, "Bouffée délirante," *Politis*, no. 1194, 15 March 2002.

31. Chevallier, "Hélène et Louis."

32. de Rabaudy, "Le fou de Franca"; Martine Silber, "Un comédien virtuose joue la folie d'Althusser," *Le Monde*, 27 November 2006, 23.

33. Contat, "Les morts d'Althusser"; Dominique Dhombres, "Grandes affaires : 1980 – le coup de folie du philosophe," *Le Monde*, 30 July 2006, 14; See also Lévy, preface, 8.

34. Annik Houel, Patricia Mercader, and Helga Sobota, *Crime passionnel, crime ordinaire* (Paris: Presses universitaires de France, 2003), 130.

35. Widmer, "Le crime d'Althusser," 17.

36. Annik Houel and Claude Tapia, "Les dessous du féminicide : le cas Althusser," *Journal des psychologues*, no. 261 (2008): 52.

37. Éric Marty, *Louis Althusser, un sujet sans procès: anatomie d'un passé très récent* (Paris: Gallimard, 1999), 16, 172.

38. Marty, *Louis Althusser*, 239.

39. Éric Marty, *Le sexe des Modernes: pensée du neutre et théorie du genre* (Paris: Éditions du Seuil, 2021).

40. Mélissa Blais, "'I Hate Feminists!': December 6, 1989, and Its Aftermath (Halifax, NS: Fernwood Publishing, 2014).

41. Althusser, *Future Lasts a Long Time*, 310.

42. Althusser, *Future Lasts a Long Time*, 295, 310.

43. Althusser, *Future Lasts a Long Time*, 3.

44. German Arce Ross, "L'homicide altruiste de Louis Althusser," *Cliniques méditerranéennes*, no, 67 (2003), 232.

45. Althusser, *Future Lasts a Long Time*, 276, emphasis in the original.

46. Jean-Paul Enthoven, "Althusser et l'amour fou," *Le Point*, no. 1367, 28 November 1998, 127.

47. The journal *L'Humanité* rips apart such explanations. See Gil Ben Aych, "Le concept de meurtre ne tue pas," *L'Humanité*, 12 May 2000, 26.

48. Roger-Pol Droit, "Le fou et le philosophe Althusser pose la question insolite et insoluble des entrelacs de la réflexion philosophique et de l'histoire des affects," *Le Monde*, 24 April 1992, 30.

49. Contat, "Les morts d'Althusser."

50. For a different opinion, see Jean-Yves Nau, "La passion d'Althusser," *Le Monde*, 27 January 1993, 11.

51. Louis B. Robitaille, "Althusser: les mémoires d'outre-tombe d'un prophète fou et meurtrier," *La Presse*, 26 April 1992, A2.

Male Protection and Solidarity

1. Virginie Ballet, "Marie Trintignant: un meurtre devenu symbole des féminicides," *Libération*, 27 July 2023, 9.

2. Alice Debauche and Christelle Hamel, "Violence des hommes contre les femmes: quelles avancées dans la production des savoirs?," *Nouvelles Questions féministes* 32, no. 1 (2013), 7.

3. Christine Delphy, "C'est le plus grand des voleurs, oui mais c'est un Gentleman," in *Un troussage de domestique* (Paris: Syllepse, 2011), 7, 12, 17.

4. Michel Dubec, "André Gide aurait-il pu juger Louis Althusser?," *Journal français de psychiatrie,* no. 13 (2001), 37.

5. Bernard-Henri Lévy, preface to *Lettres à Hélène*, by Louis Althusser, 8.

6. Louis Althusser, *The Future Lasts a Long Time: Genius, Madness, and Murder—The Extraordinary Autobiography of France's Greatest Modern Thinker*, trans. Veasey Richard (New York: Vintage, 1994)*,* 92.

7. Thomas Ferenczi, "La tolérance? Non, la justice," *Le Monde*, 2 December 1980.

8.   Althusser, *Future Lasts a Long Time*, 283.

9.   Michel Kajman, "Le combat perdu contre la déraison," *Le Monde*, 24 October 1990, 18.

10. Dominique Jamet, quoted in "Une mise au point du directeur de l'E.N.S. après la mort de Mme Althusser," *Le Monde,* 21 November 1980.

11. Annik Houel, Patricia Mercader, and Helga Sobota, *Crime passionnel, crime ordinaire* (Paris: Presses universitaires de France, 2003), 118ff.

Twist to Better Run in Circles

1.   In French, *un meurtre à deux*, a murder committed by two, is a play on the phrase *folie à deux*.

2.   Olivier Corpet, foreword in *Des rêves d'angoisse sans fin: récits de rêves (1941–1967) suivi de Un meurtre à deux (1985)*, by Louis Althusser (Paris: Grasset/IMEC, 2015), 12. Note that in this foreword, the murderer and the men in question are identified by their full or last names (Louis Althusser or Althusser) but the women are almost always identified by their first names alone (Hélène, Claire, Franca). This difference marks a hierarchy.

3.   Althusser, *Des rêves d'angoisse sans fin*, 179–81.

4.   Corpet, foreword, 11–12.

5.   Althusser, *Des rêves d'angoisse sans fin*, 210, emphasis added.

6.   Corpet, foreword, 17.

7.   Élisabeth Roudinesco, "Althusser, la raison en sommeil," *Le Monde des livres,* 25 September 2015, emphasis added.

8.   Alexis Pierçon-Gnezda, "Le monde onirique de Louis Althusser," *Les Inrocks,* 25 September 2015, emphasis added.

9.   Christophe Baconin, "Des rêves d'angoisse sans fin: Récits de rêves (1941–1967), suivi de 'Un meurtre à deux' (1985)," *Le Monde diplomatique*, February 2016, 25.

10. Corpet, foreword, 21, emphasis in the original.

11. Corpet, foreword, 19.

Lies and Glory

1.   Louis Althusser, *Des rêves d'angoisse sans fin: récits de rêves (1941–1967) suivi de Un meurtre à deux (1985)* (Paris: Grasset/IMEC, 2015), 212–13, emphasis added.

2.   In Quebec too, see Daniel Blémur, "La lutte et la vérité: la philosophie, entre histoire des sciences et intervention politique chez Michel Foucault et Louis Althusser" (PhD diss., Université de Montréal, 2017).

3.   Olivier Corpet, foreword in Althusser, *Des rêves d'angoisse sans fin*, 20.

4.   Introductory text on the Centre national des arts du cirque de la rue et du théâtre website: artcena.fr (accessed April 2023).

5.   Aliocha Wald Lasowski, "La folie ou l'astre noir qui plane: conversation avec Bernard-Henri Lévy," in *Althusser et nous* (Paris: Presses universitaires de France, 2016), 171–74.

6.   Alison Assiter, *Althusser & Feminism* (London: Pluto Press, 1990), 24.

7.   Judith Butler, "Conscience Doth Make Subjects of Us All," Yale French Studies, no. 88 (1995): 6–26, jstor.org; see also Judith Butler, *La vie psychique du pouvoir* (Paris: Léo Scheer, 2002), 174. It was after reading this text, astonishing coming from a feminist like Butler, that the idea came to me to research Hélène Legotien's murder, which then got me to delve into both the killer's and his allies' arguments.

8.   Éric Marty, *Le sexe des Modernes: pensée du Neutre et théorie du genre* (Paris: Seuil, 2021).

9.   Jacques Bidet, "Le sujet interpellé: au-delà d'Althusser et de Butler," *Actuel Marx*, no. 61 (2017), 184–201.

10.   Noela Davis, "Subjected Subjects? On Judith Butler's Paradox of Interpellation," *Hypathia* 27, no. 4 (2012).

11.   Pierre Macherey, "Judith Butler et la théorie althussérienne de l'assujettissement," *Groupe d'études "La philosophie au sens large,"* 18 February 2009, 11.

12.   Claudio Aguayo, "Butler *avec* Althusser: Notes for an

Investigation," *Décalages: A Journal of Althusser Studies* 2, no. 4 (2022): 118; Matthew Lampert, "Resisting Ideology: On Butler's Critique of Althusser," *Diacritics* 43, no. 2 (2015): 145, no. 35.

13.   Guillaume Le Blanc, "Être assujetti: Althusser, Foucault, Butler," *Actuel Marx*, no. 36 (2004): 62.

14.   See also Pierre Macherey and Stephanie Bundy, "Judith Butler and the Althusserian Theory of Subjection," *Décalages: A Journal of Althusser Studies* 1, no. 2 (2012); Won Choi, "Inception or Interpellation? The Slovenian School, Butler, and Althusser," *Rethinking Marxism* 25, no. 1 (201): 23–37; Jessica Borotto, "Interpellation du genre et sujets mélancoliques: Butler lectrice d'Althusser," *Cahiers du GRM – Groupe de recherches matérialistes*, no. 8 (2015).

15.   Hasana Sharp, "Is it Simple to Be a Feminist in Philosophy? Althusser and Feminist Theoretical Practice," *Rethinking Marxism* 12, no. 2 (2000): 18–34.

Can We Separate the Author from His Work?

1.   Francis Dupuis-Déri, "Proudhon, un anarchiste misogyne et antiféministe ou comment interpréter l'incohérence d'un auteur célèbre?," in *Antiféminismes et masculinismes d'hier et d'aujourd'hui,* eds. Christine Bard, Mélissa Blais, and Francis Dupuis-Déri (Paris: Presses universitaires de France, 2019), 79–113.

2.   William S. Lewis, *Louis Althusser and the Traditions of French Marxism* (Rowman & Littlefield, 2005); *Concrete Critical Theory: Althusser's Marxism* (Chicago: Haymarket Books, 2022); William S. Lewis, "'But Didn't He Kill His Wife?,'" in *Concrete Critical Theory: Althusser's Marxism* (Leyde, NL: Brill, 2022), 14–25.

3.   Thank you to Mathias Girel for this information.

4.   Lewis, "'But Didn't He Kill His Wife?'"

Conclusion

1. See, for example, Pierre Naville, *L'automation et le travail humain* (Paris: CNRS, 1961).
2. Hélène Legotien, "Du roman au film," *Esprit,* no. 228, July 1955, 1144, emphasis added.
3. A French nobleman convicted of art theft.
4. Claude Sarraute, "Petite faim," *Le Monde,* 14 March 1985.
5. Vania Widmer, "Le crime d'Althusser," *L'Écrit,* no. 54 (2004): 19.
6. Louis Althusser, *The Future Lasts a Long Time: Genius, Madness, and Murder—The Extraordinary Autobiography of France's Greatest Modern Thinker,* trans. Veasey Richard (New York: Vintage, 1994), 8.
7. Althusser, *Future Lasts a Long Time.*
8. Widmer, "Le crime d'Althusser," 18–19.
9. Jalna Hanmer, "Violence et contrôle social des femmes," *Questions féministes,* no. 1 (1977).

Epilogue: The Spectre of Hélène Legotien

1. Thank you to everyone quoted here for allowing me to share their words.
2. Mathilde Larrère, *Rage against the machisme* (Éditions du Détour, 2020).
3. Johanna Luyssen, "Louis Althusser et Hélène Rytmann: Le philosophe assassin et le féminicide occulté," *Libération,* 26 December 2023, 2–4.
4. Lucie Rondeau du Noyer, "La deuxième vie d'Hélène Legotien," *Les Carnets de l'IMEC,* no. 22 (Autumn 2024): 34–35.
5. Valérie Lefebvre-Faucher, *Jenny, Eleanor, Laura, et al: This Is Not a Book About Marx,* trans. Mélissa Bull (Between the Lines, 2025), 70.
6. See his book *Cécile et Marx. Héritages de liens et de luttes* (Varia, 2024).

7.   "Texte de Louis Althusser sur le 'mouvement des femmes,'" IMEC – Althusser Collection, 2OALT 28.7.

8.   Louis Althusser, "On Conjugal Obscenity (1951)," in *Écrits philosophiques et politiques, Tome 1* (Stock/IMEC, 1994).

9.   I would like to refer to the article co-written with Mélissa Blais, "Masculinism and the Antifeminist Countermovement," *Social Movement Studies* 11, no. 1 (2012): 21–39; and to my text "Castratrices! Archétype antiféministe du XIXe au XXe siècle (France et Québec)," in *Castrations: Testicules et masculinités,* ed. Nahema Hanafi (Le Murmure, 2024).